ARE LEADERS BORN
OR ARE THEY MADE?

Detail: Alexander sarcophagus, Istanbul Archaeological Museum

ARE LEADERS BORN OR ARE THEY MADE?

The Case of Alexander the Great

Manfred F. R. Kets de Vries
with
Elisabet Engellau

KARNAC
LONDON   NEW YORK

First published in 2003 in Dutch:
Het Leiderschap van Alexander de Grote
by Uitgeverij Nieuwezijds

English edition published in 2004 by
H. Karnac (Books) Ltd.
6 Pembroke Buildings, London NW10 6RE

British Library Cataloguing in Publication Data

A C.I.P. for this book is available from the British Library

ISBN 1 85575 315 4

Edited, designed and produced by The Studio Publishing Services Ltd, Exeter EX4 8JN

Printed in Great Britain

10 9 8 7 6 5 4 3 2 1

www.karnacbooks.com

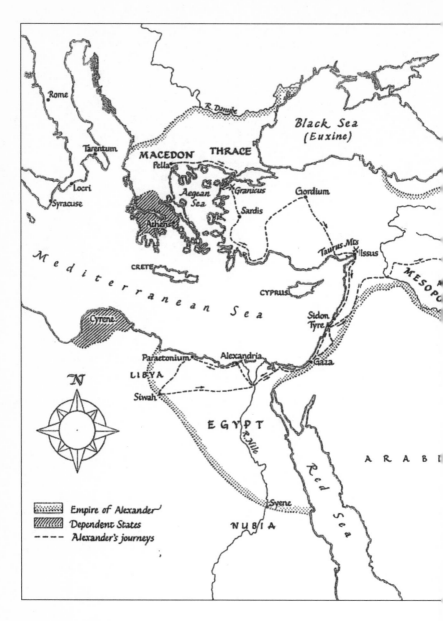

Alexander's Empire

The Empire of Alexander the Great

Caspian Sea

Aral Sea

R. Jaxartes

R. Oxus

Samarkand

SOGDIANA

BACTRIA

Hindu Kush

MEDIA

HYRCANIA

PARTHIA

R. Indus

R. Hydaspes

Susa

Alexandria

Persepolis

PERSIS

ARACHOSIA

R. Indus

Persian Gulf

GEDROSIA

Erythraean Sea

500 km

500 miles

CONTENTS

LIST OF ILLUSTRATIONS

ABOUT THE AUTHORS

Manfred F. R. Kets de Vries brings a different view to the much studied subjects of leadership and the dynamics of individual and organizational change. Bringing to bear his knowledge and experience of economics (Econ. Drs., University of Amsterdam), management (ITP, MBA, and DBA, Harvard Business School), and psychoanalysis (Canadian Psychoanalytic Society and the International Psychoanalytic Association), he probes the interface between international management, psychoanalysis, psychotherapy, and dynamic psychiatry. His specific areas of interest are leadership, career dynamics, executive stress, entrepreneurship, family business, succession planning, cross-cultural management, and the dynamics of corporate transformation and change.

A clinical professor of leadership development, he holds the Raoul de Vitry d'Avaucourt Chair of Leadership Development at INSEAD, Fontainebleau, France and Singapore. He is director of INSEAD's Global Leadership Centre. He is director of INSEAD's top management programme, "The Challenge of Leadership: Developing Your Emotional Intelligence" and of "Consulting and Coaching for Change" (and has five times received INSEAD's distinguished teacher award). He has also held professorships at

McGill University, the Ecole des Hautes Etudes Commerciales, Montreal, and the Harvard Business School, and he has lectured at management institutions around the world. He is a founding member of the International Society for the Psychoanalytic Study of Organizations. *The Financial Times, Le Capital, Wirtschaftswoche,* and *The Economist* have judged Manfred Kets de Vries one of the world's leading management thinkers.

Kets de Vries is the author, co-author, or editor of twenty books, including *Power and the Corporate Mind* (1975, new edition 1985, with Abraham Zaleznik), *Organizational Paradoxes: Clinical Approaches to Management* (1980, new edition 1994), *The Irrational Executive: Psychoanalytic Explorations in Management* (1984, editor), *The Neurotic Organization: Diagnosing and Changing Counter-Productive Styles of Management* (1984, new edition 1990, with Danny Miller), *Unstable at the Top* (1988, with Danny Miller), *Prisoners of Leadership* (1989), *Handbook of Character Studies* (1991, with Sidney Perzow), *Organizations on the Couch* (1991), *Leaders, Fools and Impostors* (1993, new edition 2003), the prize-winning *Life and Death in the Executive Fast Lane: Essays on Organizations and Leadership* (1995) (the Critics' Choice Award 1995–1996), *Family Business: Human Dilemmas in the Family Firm* (1996), *The New Global Leaders: Percy Barnevik, Richard Branson, and David Simon* (1999, with Elizabeth Florent), *Struggling with the Demon: Perspectives on Individual and Organizational Irrationality* (2001), *The Leadership Mystique* (2001), *The Happiness Equation* (2002), and *The Global Executive Leadership Inventory* (2004). Recently, two new books have been finished, one on the new Russian leaders and one on the psychology of leadership by terror.

In addition, Kets de Vries has published over 200 scientific papers as chapters in books and as articles in such journals as *Behavioral Science, Journal of Management Studies, Human Relations, Administration & Society, Organizational Dynamics, Strategic Management Journal, Academy of Management Journal, Academy of Management Review, Journal of Forecasting, California Management Review, Harvard Business Review, Sloan Management Review, Academy of Management Executive, Psychoanalytic Review, Bulletin of the Menninger Clinic, Journal of Applied Behavioral Science, European Management Journal, International Journal of Cross Cultural Management, Harper's* and *Psychology Today.* He has also written over a hundred case studies, including seven that received the Best Case of the

Year award. He is a regular writer for a number of magazines. His work has been featured in such publications as *The New York Times*, *The Wall Street Journal*, *The Los Angeles Times*, *Fortune*, *Business Week*, *The Economist*, *The Financial Times*, and *The International Herald Tribune*. His books and articles have been translated into eighteen languages. He is a member of seventeen editorial boards. He has been elected a Fellow of the Academy of Management.

Kets de Vries is a consultant on organizational design/transformation and strategic human resource management to leading American, Canadian, European, African, and Asian companies. As a global consultant in executive development his clients have included ABB, Aegon, Air Liquide, Alcan, Alcatel, Accenture, Bain Consulting, Bang & Olufsen, Bonnier, BP, Ericsson, GE Capital, Goldman Sachs, Heineken, HypoVereinsbank, Investec, KPMG, Lego, Lundbeck Lufthansa, Novartis, Nokia, NovoNordisk, Rank Xerox, Shell, SHV, Standard Bank of South Africa, Unilever, Vodafone and Volvo Car Corporation. As an educator and consultant he has worked in more than thirty countries.

The Dutch government has made him an Officer in the Order of Oranje Nassau. He was the first fly fisherman in Outer Mongolia and is a member of New York's Explorers' Club. In his spare time he can be found in the rainforests or savannas of Central Africa, the Siberian taiga, the Pamir mountains, or within the Arctic circle.

Elisabet Engellau is Adjunct Clinical Professor of Management at INSEAD (Fontainebleau/Singapore). As Programme Director at INSEAD's Global Leadership Centre, she focuses on leadership development and coaching in executive programmes, open enrolment, as well as company specific programmes. In addition, she regularly serves as visiting faculty at the Center for Creative Leadership, and the Stockholm School of Economics. She has been an affiliate professor at McGill University's Faculty of Management, and a teaching fellow at Harvard University and Concordia University, Montreal. She has also produced and directed a number of video films for management education and has recently been involved in developing two new feedback instruments.

Ms Engellau also works as an independent consultant, specializing in one-on-one executive coaching, leadership development, cross-cultural management and team building. Her professional activities are focused on the dynamics of corporate transformation and change. In her work with individuals and teams in major European and multi-national organizations such as ABN-AMRO, Bain, CIBA, Deutsche Bank, Goldman Sachs, HypoVereinsbank, Lundbeck, Nokia, Standard Bank of South Africa, Vodafone, Unilever and The Cabinet Office, UK, she combines her long-term interest in creativity with a clinical approach to human resource management.

Her previous professional experience includes production and management in a variety of creative fields in an international context. She has held management positions at the Royal Opera of Stockholm, the Museum of Modern Art, Stockholm, and Malmö Municipal Theatre.

She has pursued academic studies at Uppsala University (MA in Art History, Literature and Anthropology), at Harvard University (graduate work in Psychology and Social Studies) and at McGill University (PhD studies in Communications and Management) and has undertaken psychoanalytic training in Montreal and Paris.

She is a member of the Research Group on Leadership Practices, The International Society for the Psychoanalytic Study of Organizations (ISPSO), The American Psychological Association (APA) and Institut de Psychoanalyse & Management (IPM).

Ms Engellau has a great interest in the arts as well as the outdoors (she has been a line record holder of the *hucho taimen* in Outer Mongolia).

PREFACE

During the heyday of the internet bubble I was often approached by journalists wondering what was new about leadership in the "New Economy". My usual response was that it was not really a new economy at all, but an old economy with a new technology. I tried to explain to them that many of the soundest principles of leadership are very old. I pointed out, for example, that many of the principles of leadership from the time of Alexander the Great still apply. I reminded the journalists that the pursuit of glory is a timeless activity. From ancient to modern history, glory has been a rallying cry. As Napoleon Bonaparte is supposed to have said, "Glory is fleeting, but obscurity is forever!"

After I had given this response numerous times to questions about new forms of leadership, I decided that I should make a more in-depth investigation into Alexander the Great's leadership style. Perhaps I would discover that my responses to questions about leadership in the new economy had been too flippant. And so I immersed myself in the story of Alexander. One book on Alexander led to another, and another, and another, as I became entranced by his life story. Alexander's exploits had captured the imagination of countless scholars and laymen, and now they had me too.

Exploring Alexander's life was a fascinating journey into the history of leadership. To my surprise, that journey also took me down memory lane. I remembered how as a child I was intrigued by the story of the Gordian knot—a knot so entangled that legend said the person who could untie it would become ruler over all of Asia. What spoke to a child's imagination was Alexander's deft solution: he cut the knot. Another (perhaps apocryphal) story that stayed with me from childhood told of Alexander weeping because there were no more worlds to conquer.

To me, as both child and adult, this conqueror represents the dictum that there is nothing impossible for those who persevere.

Alexander the Great: ivory from the royal grave in Vergina, Macedonia

Alexander is an example of unlimited ambition, of desiring to have it *all*—and then working relentlessly to achieve that ambition. Like Julius Caesar, he could say, of all the places he travelled, *Veni, vidi, vici* ("I came, I saw, I conquered"). He was a man with a dream, a dreamer who spoke to the collective imagination of humankind. And as William Shakespeare observed in *Hamlet*, "Dreams indeed are ambition. For the very substance of the ambitious is merely the shadow of a dream."

For her help in getting this small book project off the ground, I would like to thank my wife and collaborator, Elisabet Engellau. With her background in art history, she made this journey into the origins of leadership aesthetically more appealing. Playing the role of Dante's Beatrice, she helped me select visual imagery that strengthened the text. In addition, her deep understanding of the psychology of leadership made her a formidable and constructive critic in the development of this book. Because her contribution was considerable, I have listed her as a co-author.

In the development of this book I would also like to thank the participants of the two leadership seminars I run at INSEAD: the top-management seminar, "The Challenge of Leadership: Developing Your Emotional Intelligence", and a more recent arrival, "Coaching and Consulting for Change". The contributions made by my participants while testing certain assumptions about leadership were invaluable. During the dialogue with the participants I discovered that in many ways, life is just like a mirror: perception is coloured by the reality you find inside yourself. I would also like to thank my other collaborators at INSEAD's Global Leadership Centre: Sudhir Kakar, Roger Lehman, and Erik van der Loo.

I would like to express my gratitude to INSEAD for providing me with the time and space to investigate what, at least for business schools, are unusual research topics. Members of the research department and committee—particularly Anil Gaba, Landir Gabel, and Allison James—have always been extremely helpful, supporting me in my research activities. My personal assistant, Sheila Loxham, has a remarkable ability to manage someone who at times can be quite unmanageable. I appreciate that ability and her consummate good cheer: she always looks at the bright side. My research project manager, Elizabeth Florent, has created a working environment for our leadership research group that allows me to devote a considerable amount of my time to writing. I would also like to thank my irrepressible editor, Kathy Reigstad, who has been invaluable in transforming my rather Germanic syntax into more palatable reading material. Over the years, she has taught me much about grammar, although I suspect she has forgotten more than I will ever learn.

Writing remains a journey into the interior. Biases—perceptual and emotional distortions—are very much a part of this process. What I have written about Alexander in this book is only *opinion*. Though much has been said about him, much remains concealed. And as is the case so often with men and women of renown, to be great is to be misunderstood!

Manfred F. R. Kets de Vries
Paris, France

INTRODUCTION

Personally, I have no data from which to infer precisely what Alexander had in mind, and I do not care to make guesses: one thing, however, I feel I can say without fear of contradiction, and that is that his plans, whatever they were, had no lack of grandeur or ambition: he would never have remained idle in the enjoyment of any of his conquests, even had he extended his empire from Asia to Europe to the British Isles. On the contrary, he would have continued to seek beyond them for unknown lands, as it was ever his nature, if he had no rival, to strive to better his own best. [Arrian,*The Campaigns of Alexander* (pp. 348–349)

True contentment depends not on what we have; a tub was large enough for Diogenes, but a world was too little for Alexander. [Charles Colton, *Lacon*]

Alexander the Great was psychologically of the same type as the lunatic, though he possessed the talent to achieve the lunatic's dream. [Bertrand Russell, *The Conquest of Happiness*]

The objective of this book is to study the psychodynamics of leadership—in other words, to explore the mindset of the leader.

To gain a better understanding of what effective leadership is all about, this book looks at one specific notable leader's inner theatre—that of Alexander the Great of Macedonia, one of the most famous leaders of all time. In his short life Alexander conquered a territory that now spans modern Turkey, Lebanon, Israel, Egypt, Syria, Iraq, Iran, Afghanistan, and part of India. His life-story illustrates the psychological forces that generally come into play in the making of a leader. It is those forces, and the episodes in his life that give most insight into his personality, that this book focuses on, leaving the details of his life to the myriad books and articles that have been written about him.[1]

In analysing Alexander's personality and behaviour, this book takes a clinical perspective. It relies on concepts of developmental psychology, family systems theory, cognitive theory, dynamic psychiatry, psychotherapy, and psychoanalysis to understand his behaviour and actions. Exploring themes that highlight psychological dimensions of Alexander's leadership style, these pages draw observations about the lessons of leadership that can be learned from his behaviour.

Note

1. Saying something new about Alexander the Great poses a mighty challenge, because more than 30,000 books and articles have been written on the subject over time, new volumes appearing at the rate of at least one a year. Complicating the study of Alexander even further is the fact that although more than twenty of his contemporaries wrote books about the great king, none of them has survived. The existence of these books is known only from references and quotations by later authors, who may not have been true to the original wording.

PART I
HISTIOGRAPHY

Alexander as the son of Zeus-Ammon: coin, Fitzwilliam Museum, Cambridge

CHAPTER ONE

Setting the stage

Alexander the Great, one of the greatest generals of all time and one of the most powerful personalities of antiquity, was born in 356 BC in Pella, Macedonia (Baynham, 1998; Bosworth, 1988; Bury & Meiggs, 1983; Freeman, 1999; Green, 1991; Hammond, 1998; Hogarth, 1977; Lamb, 1945; Stewart, 1993). Although the Macedonians, whose territory occupied the area around present-day Thessaloniki in northern Greece, considered themselves part of the Greek cultural sphere, many Greeks regarded them with contempt. In the eyes of the Greeks, the Macedonians were a mere offshoot of the original stock. They spoke a Greek dialect, to be sure, but they were led by a backward monarchy and their nobles (little more than barbarians) pursued the manly pleasures of hunting, drinking, frolicking, and casual fornication, the latter quite indiscriminately with both men and women.

Parental disharmony

In 359 BC, King Perdiccas III, then ruler of Macedonia, died in battle. His infant son, Amyntas, was expected to succeed him, with

1

Perdiccas's brother Philip (Alexander the Great's father) as his regent. Philip, however, usurped his nephew's throne, crowning himself King Philip II. With that bold step he set the stage for the meteoric rise of his country's fortunes and its entry on to the world stage (Cawkwell, 1981).

King Philip, who had been educated by Epaminondas (the finest military strategist of Greece before Alexander), was a brilliant ruler and strategist. In just a few decades he conquered most of Greece. He was fortunate in that Macedonia was rich in gold and silver mines—particularly as the empire expanded—giving him financial clout that was matched only by King Darius of Persia. These riches enabled him to maintain a formidable mercenary force and to bribe senior officials in the various surrounding kingdoms and city-states when it suited his political purposes.

As the ruler of his country, King Philip exercised absolute control over Macedonian affairs. He was an astute politician with a good sense of *realpolitik* and a knack for playing politicians off against one another. The fact that he was able to transform

King Philip: relief on gold medallion, third century BC

Macedonia from a backwater to one of the most powerful states in the Greek world was a tribute to his commanding personality, his talents as a diplomat, and his exceptional skill as a general.

Alexander's mother, Olympias, was the orphaned daughter of King Neoptolemus of Epirus, an area located in what is now Albania. In the fall of 357 BC she married Philip in a union arranged for political purposes, an alliance intended to safeguard a relationship with a potentially troublesome neighbour.

Olympias was beautiful, but she was possessed by a terrible temper and wilfulness which, when coupled with her great intelligence, made her an extremely difficult and complex person to live with. According to the documentation of the time, Olympias could be cruel, stubborn, headstrong, sullen, and meddlesome. She rarely either hid or restrained her emotions and was prone to mood swings, ranging often from one extreme of feeling to another. Her quarrelsome temper put her at war with Philip (and him at war with her) for most of Alexander's childhood.

Queen Olympias: relief on gold medallion, third century BC

Olympias, having been initiated into the cults of Dionysus, was an eager devotee of mystic rituals and torch-lit fertility rites. Her frequent participation in Maenadic frenzies added to the turmoil in Alexander's home life. As a devoted Bacchant, she often led the processions herself, sacrificing animals and drinking their blood. Among the more bizarre habits noted by her contemporaries, she kept an assortment of snakes for religious rites all over the place, including in her bed—an endeavour that must have discouraged conjugal visits by her husband (Plutarch, 1973). These strange habits led Philip (and his entourage), who were subject to the many superstitions of that age, to wonder whether she was perhaps an enchantress, possessing dangerous magical powers.

Tradition tells that Olympias was descended from Achilles, the mythical hero of the *Iliad*, while Alexander's father, Philip II of Macedonia, was said to descend from Zeus's son Heracles. Both Olympias and Philip had dreams foretelling Alexander's conception, and these dreams seem to bear out the regal heritage. Legend tells that soon after the marriage Olympias dreamed that she was impregnated by a thunderbolt as fire flooded her body (later spreading out across the earth). (According to popular myth, Zeus was the wielder of thunderbolts.) In King Philip's dream he sealed her womb with the image of a lion. The most renowned seer of that time was invited to interpret their dreams (so the legend continues), and he concluded that Olympias was pregnant and that the child would have the character of a lion (Arrian, 1971; Lane Fox, 1994).

In keeping with Macedonian tradition, Philip had four lesser wives and many mistresses. (Diplomat that he was, he was said to take a new wife with every war in an effort to secure the boundaries of his kingdom through political marriages that showed his goodwill towards kingdoms worth conciliating.) Although Olympias could accept his affairs with women (and even men), she would not have brooked any threat to her position as the reigning queen—the queen-mother-to-be—and to her son's position as the crown prince and future king. Any hazard to this position incurred her murderous temper. She had a reputation for ruthlessness and seemed prepared to dispose of her enemies if necessary. Philip and Olympias had one more child together, a daughter named Cleopatra. Thereafter, it can be assumed (given their conflict-ridden relationship), sexual intercourse ceased.

Queen Olympias's only real love—a love that was total and all-consuming—was for her only son. She was often jealous, vindictive, and extremely protective of Alexander, who would idolize his mother as long as he lived. While her son was growing up, she made sure that many of the people in his inner circle were associated with *her* family. She wanted him to be part of *her* camp, not that of her husband. As a devotee of mystic rituals she honoured the gods on a daily basis, a practice emulated by her son. Consequently, Alexander grew up profoundly religious, primed to believe in the manifestation of gods in many cults and places. Steeped in Homer, he lived in a world of Greek heroes and gods. Throughout his life he would always be looking for divine signs to lead him on his way; and Dionysian rites in particular fascinated him, a result of his mother's influence.

Alexander's religious interest was fuelled by Olympias's stories (told out of spite when her relationship with Philip began to deteriorate) that his true father was not Philip but Zeus, king of the gods, a tale that spoke to the imagination of the young boy. Later, Alexander traced his ancestry to the demi-god Heracles, the most popular of Greek heroes. Heracles was famous for his extraordinary strength and courage, as demonstrated in his performance of twelve arduous labours, including the killing of the Nemean lion.

Education

Compared to the Macedonian traditions of his day, Alexander received a highly sophisticated education. Until the age of thirteen he stayed at home, initially under the care of his nurse, Lanice (sister of Cleitus the Black, the commander of the royal squadron of the Companion Cavalry). Then, at the age of seven, he stepped out from under her wing to undergo rigorous training by Leonidas, a relative of Olympias. This kinsman taught him the physical skills needed for being a warrior king—skills such as horse riding and sword fighting. Contemporaries of Alexander tell that the youth displayed great aptitude for sports and combat. He also learned the virtues of self-control and self-denial during this early stage (Arrian, 1971; Bosworth, 1988).

Stern, petty, and controlling, Leonidas was in the habit of searching Alexander's possessions to ensure that Olympias had not smuggled any luxuries to her son. Spoiling children was not part of his educational programme. He instilled in Alexander the ascetic nature for which he became famous during his future campaigns: for much of his short adult life he would live spartanly, eating and sleeping together with his troops.

During Alexander's training with Leonidas, the young prince is said to have extravagantly thrown two fistfuls of incense on the altar fire during a religious ceremony. Leonidas, so the story goes, chided him, saying, "When you have conquered the spice-bearing regions, you can throw away all the incense you like. Till then, do not waste it" (Plutarch, 1973, p. 281). That admonition stuck with the young man. Many years later, after he captured Gaza, the main spice depot for the whole Middle East, Alexander sent Leonidas eighteen tons of frankincense and myrrh with the admonition not to be so stingy towards the gods (Green, 1991; Plutarch, 1973).

During his early military training, Alexander was also taught by the courtier Lysimachus, a person with very different interests from those of Leonidas. Lysimachus helped Alexander appreciate the arts and taught him to play the lyre. Lysimachus was much beloved by Alexander and liked to call himself Phoenix to Alexander's Achilles. Later in life, encouraged by his teacher, Alexander would be a great patron of musicians, actors, painters, writers, and architects.

Because of Lysimachus's influence, Alexander is said to have known the writings of Homer and Euripides by heart. He had a great love for Homer's epic sagas and was inspired by the mighty deeds of the gods and heroes during the Trojan War. He always slept with a copy of the *Iliad* under his pillow. His favourite line from Homer is said to have been, "Ever to be the best and stand far above all others." His favourite role model was the *Iliad*'s Achilles (in part, presumably, because of the assumed familial link).

As portrayed in works of antiquity, even as a young boy Alexander was fearless, strong, tempestuous, and eager to learn. Father and son were both extremely ambitious and highly competitive. Alexander was like a racehorse, eager to emulate and then surpass the conquests of his father. As a youngster, he is said to have complained to his friends, "My father will forestall me in everything. There will be nothing great or spectacular for you and me to show the world" (Plutarch, 1973, p. 256). In spite of the spirit of competition between the two of them, however, Philip was immensely proud of his precocious son—at least initially.

At the age of twelve, Alexander tamed the beautiful and spirited Bucephalus (meaning "ox-head" in Greek), a horse that no one else (including his father) was courageous enough to ride. Always ready for a dare, and compelled to compete with his father, he made a wager that he would be able to ride the horse. His father—who feared for his son's life when he tried to tame the stallion—is said to have wept for joy when the boy returned triumphantly seated on the horse. After this feat his father allegedly said, "You must find a kingdom big enough for your ambitions. Macedonia is too small for

Alexander astride Bucephalus: Hellenistic bronze, Herculanum

you" (Plutarch, 1973, p. 258). Eventually, this famous stallion carried him as far the Hydaspes River in India, where the mount died. In sorrow, Alexander built the city of Bucephala, in memory of his beloved horse.

As time passed, Alexander's relationship with his father became increasingly discordant. When his father began to slight his mother, Alexander clung to the fantasy that Philip was not his real father, that he had a more regal ancestry as a child of the gods. Olympias fed this fantasy and also encouraged Alexander to think of himself as a king in his own right, not merely a successor to Philip. This frame of mind, and the behaviours it engendered, led to many father–son quarrels.

When Alexander reached the age of thirteen, his father felt that it was time for the young man to move on to higher education. King Philip chose the still relatively unknown philosopher Aristotle to work with his son. For three years Alexander and the other boys of the Macedonian aristocracy (known collectively as the School of Pages) were taught by Aristotle at the Mieza temple, about thirty kilometres from the royal palace at Pella. Among this select group of aristocrats were his lifelong friend and lover Hephaestion, Cassander, son of the general Antipater, and Ptolemy, the two last being themselves future kings.

In this "miniature Academy" Aristotle introduced Alexander to the world of arts and sciences. Alexander developed a great aptitude for debate, rhetoric, and drama during these years, becoming a gifted orator who could tailor his message to any situation (a faculty that would be extremely helpful later, when he led his troops). His tutor also stimulated his passion for scientific exploration and discovery. Due to the influence of Aristotle, Alexander developed a strong interest in medicine, botany, and zoology. Later, his knowledge of medicine would stand him in good stead, lending understanding to his concern for his soldiers' wounds and sicknesses.

In addition, Aristotle's political teachings provided Alexander with a solid background in law and statecraft, profoundly influencing the young prince and preparing him for the administration of his later empire. Aristotle wrote the treatise *On Kingship* (a document that has not survived the centuries) to help Alexander understand his responsibilities. The philosopher's image of the

Aristotle: National Museum, Rome

philosopher-king gave the future king a role model he could
emulate. As Aristotle conquered the world with thought, he taught
the young man who would conquer the world with the sword
(Aristotle, 1988).

CHAPTER TWO

Creating a war machine

Until the fifth century BC Greek warfare had been a matter of amateur civilian armies going on summer campaigns. Soldiering had been a part-time occupation, something men would do during the off-season. At the start of the harvest the men would return to their farms. This arrangement was gradually changing, however.

Philip as military innovator

In Philip's fourth century BC, warfare was becoming more and more the business of specialist professional mercenaries. Poverty drove many men from all parts of Greece to join the military, since hiring oneself out as a soldier was a good way of making a living in a poor country (especially if one had slaves who could cultivate the land). The members of the king's own regiment—an elite corps whose members were required to hold citizenship as Macedonians—were called the king's "Companions". From these soldiers, drawn from the noble families in Macedonia, Philip would select his commanders and administrators. These noblemen were divided into two categories—Cavalry Companions and Infantry Companions—each with their own fighting speciality.

Philip made the military a way of life for many Macedonian men. At great cost to the treasury, he made soldiering an occupation that paid well enough to be undertaken by his citizens year-round. He transformed his army from a body that was little more than a weak, undisciplined amateur force into a tough, disciplined war machine. To improve the soldiers' physical fitness, he insisted on frequent exercises under arms and arranged physical competitions. He was the first Greek commander to recognize the need for close cooperation between cavalry and infantry, the role of military engineers, the importance of military reconnaissance, and the advantages of speed of action. Philip's military innovations created the fighting power that Alexander inherited and perfected, making it an unsurpassed war machine (Ashley, 1997). If Philip had not had such a remarkable son, he probably would have been known as the most brilliant general of antiquity.

Philip was also a military innovator in weaponry and strategy. The Greek and Macedonian soldiers of the day wore helmets, breastplates, steel-ribbed skirts, and greaves to protect their lower legs. Although only officers initially wore a metal cuirass, under Alexander's reign every infantryman eventually was provided with this form of body protection. Each man had a solid round shield, bossed with metal, and they huddled together in echelon so that their shields overlapped. When in battle position, there was little to be seen of a man from the front except armour.

Philip also introduced the *sarissa*, a five- to seven-metre-long wooden pike with a sharp iron point, for use by his infantry for "remote" killing. This tool, used in combination with the aforementioned overlapping echelons, resulted in the celebrated "Macedonian phalanx", an impenetrable fighting wall that advanced ruthlessly into enemy lines. The *sarissa*, when held upright by the rear rows of the phalanx, helped hide manoeuvres behind the phalanx from the view of the enemy. When held horizontal by the front rows of the phalanx, it was a brutal weapon.

The men of each division were arranged in combinations of 256 men (sixteen men wide and sixteen men deep), carefully spaced, each man placed so that he might cover the gaps between his neighbours, using his helmet, breastplate, and shield as a portion of the

Macedonian phalanx: detail of painting by Jean-Paul Cleren

communal armour plate. The whole array—each man bearing a pike—would bear down on an enemy line as a terrifying blade of steel, all the while shouting the terrifying war cry "Alalalalai!" As part of the phalanx, the Macedonian soldiers were drilled to turn in any direction (changing when necessary the depth of their placement) and to reach out between as many as five rows of their comrades to plunge that iron point into the bellies of approaching enemies. People could be stabbed from six metres away, creating quite an advantage over traditional hand-to-hand combat. The combination of spears and armour was the most impersonal agent for killing adversaries that the ancient world had discovered.

In addition to the basic phalanx, Philip (and later Alexander) used lightly armed, extremely mobile auxiliaries—the Royal Shield-bearers (the finest foot force in antiquity)—archers, a siege train, and cavalry. With all of these troops perfectly coordinated in their execution, both Philip and Alexander were unbeatable. The cavalry was often deployed for reconnaissance and for lightning strikes. King Philip also helped Alexander understand the value of his corps of engineers in the development of new methods of siege warfare. Alexander revolutionized such techniques to great success.

Wielding the *sarissa* and maintaining the formation of the phalanx required extensive training and physical fitness on the part of every soldier. By making the military a full-time occupation, Philip was able to drill his men regularly, building unity and cohesion within the army. Training (and more training), combined with real combat experience, enabled the Macedonian army to operate with lightning speed and deadly efficiency. Alexander learned to appreciate fighting with the finest military machine that Greece and Asia had ever seen. And although Philip may have been the creator, Alexander became the maestro of this fighting machine.

Military training in practice

During Philip's expedition against Byzantium in 340 BC, when Alexander was sixteen years old, he left his son to serve as regent of Macedonia. To deal with an uprising during Philip's absence, Alexander led an expedition to a wild region of what is now Bulgaria. He and his troops managed to subjugate the rebellious Maedi, a Thracian tribe, and he established his first city (of many to come), Alexandropolis, imitating Philip's creation of Philippopolis, the name given to a similar outpost after a recent victory.

After this triumph his father made him a general in the army. But in spite of his remarkable achievements at such a young age, things remained tense between father and son. On one occasion when the two were fighting side-by-side during another battle of the Thracian campaign, Philip was injured. He fell to the ground and played dead while Alexander shielded him and fought off his attackers. Yet, according to historical sources, Philip never acknowledged that Alexander had saved his life, a fact that Alexander deeply resented (Fildes & Fletcher, 2001).

Philip's main conquest was that of the Greek mainland. His vision was to create a "Hellenic community", a defensive alliance among the quarrelling Greek city-states and Macedonia that would be strong enough to overpower the Great King Darius of Asia Minor and liberate the Greeks there. Philip's so-called League of Corinth, established in 337 BC, was designed to preserve and perpetuate a general peace, inaugurated when the delegates of all the states of Greece (except Sparta) and the islands swore to abide by it and to recognize Philip as president (*hegemon*) for this purpose. Such a league was a political innovation: before the creation of this agreement, peace had never lasted long, because the leading Greek states had neither the power nor the mutual trust to create an effective organization for collective action against aggressors.

Many of the politicians of the city-states remained opposed to the idea of a Greek community even after the league's inception, seeing it as a violation of their independence. In Thebes, for example, resistance to the union was strong. At the battle at Chaeronea in Boeotia in August of 338 BC Alexander was put in charge of the Macedonian cavalry, and he led a victorious attack against the Theban "Sacred Band", a group of soldiers that had never before been defeated. This contribution was instrumental in the decisive battle at Chaeronea, in which Philip defeated the allied Greek states. In spite of his success, Alexander felt that his father insufficiently appreciated his role against their formidable enemy. His demonstration of strength and courage won Alexander much popularity and respect among the Macedonian soldiers, however. This popularity would be his greatest ally when, at the age of twenty, Alexander would witness the murder of his father. After the battle at Chaeronea, Macedonians began to speak of Philip as their general and of Alexander as their king, an interpretation that did not please Philip.

With the Greek city-states firmly toeing the line, Philip began to prepare himself for his Persian campaign, with the objective of liberating the Greek cities of Asia Minor from Persian rule. Panhellenism had become his new credo. He portrayed the planned campaign as a religious crusade that would punish Persia for past wrongdoings, avenging Greece for the invasion by Xerxes more than a century before. To get this campaign under way, he shipped an advance force into Asia Minor but he (ominously) did not give his son a command position. This act was interpreted by Alexander as a major slight.

Because this was an age of omens, Philip sent enquiries to the oracle of Delphi asking whether he would conquer the Persian king. The response of the oracle was, "The bull is garlanded. All is done. The sacrificer is ready" (Diodorus, 1992, 16. 91. 2). King Philip interpreted these words as confirmation of imminent success. He was wrong, however; as it turned out, he was the one who was going to be sacrificed.

CHAPTER THREE

Family turmoil

The family was irreparably split apart when Philip took a girl younger than Alexander for his new wife. This girl, pregnant with a child by Philip, divided the royal house into two bitterly hostile camps because of her family connections. Her family was of pure Macedonian lineage, and her uncle, Attalus, was one of the Companions of the king. By taking a wife from this family, Philip had endangered the succession plans of Olympias and Alexander. Because the new wife was of traditional Macedonian nobility (unlike Alexander's mother, who came from Epirus), Olympias and Alexander were deeply threatened by his father siring a child with purer Macedonian blood than Alexander's own. Compounding the problem for Olympias, Philip renamed his new wife Eurydice, after his beloved mother, a woman who had been held in highest honour. That was a sure sign of the demotion of the queen-mother-to-be. Olympias and Alexander must have felt that the faction that surrounded Attalus undermined their position, resulting in an atmosphere of insecurity and distrust at the Macedonian court.

An incident at Philip's wedding ceremony caused an outright rupture. The bride's uncle toasted the couple, saying that he hoped his niece would give birth to a "legitimate" heir to the throne. Alexander's response was predictable, given his temper (and not being a stranger to heavy drinking himself): he is said to have hurled his cup at Attalus and shouted, "Villain, do you take me for a bastard, then?" (Plutarch, 1973, p. 261). Attalus threw his own cup back, and a general brawl ensued. History does not record what they said next, but the fight was enough to infuriate Philip. According to various sources, he stood up enraged, pulled his sword, and lunged at Alexander, only to trip and fall on his face in a drunken stupor. "Look, men," Alexander sneered, "here is the man who was making ready to cross from Europe to Asia, and who cannot even cross from one table to another without losing his balance" (Hogarth, 1977; Plutarch, 1973, p. 261).

This incident caused a rift between Philip and Alexander that sent Alexander racing with his friends and mother across the border into Epirus, the land of Olympias's birth. Alexander left his mother in the royal house of Epirus and sped on to Illyria, possibly to foment rebellion against his father. Later he reconciled with Philip and returned home, but he continued to mistrust his father. They had become a family in name only. The relationship between father and son remained strained and would never be the same again.

Regicide

When the satrap (governor) of Caria in the Persian Empire, was trying to marry his daughter to Philip's retarded son, Arridaeus, Alexander feared that Philip intended to make Arridaeus— Alexander's half-brother—his successor. That he should believe such a rumour is indicative of Alexander's increasing insecurity about his position in his father's eyes. (Philip's new wife had given birth to a daughter and was again with child.) In a panic, Alexander secretly schemed to marry the satrap's daughter himself. Philip learned of the plot before it was carried out, however, and placed Alexander under house arrest. He also banished most of Alexander's friends from the kingdom and planned to divorce Olympias, who had encouraged the plot. Always the ultimate politician, he placated Olympias's brother (the king of Epirus), by offering him his daughter's hand in marriage, despite the fact that Cleopatra was the king's niece. This marriage offer, accepted by the Epirian king, was flatly against the interest of Olympias, who was the bride's mother and the bridegroom's sister. Creating this new alliance would be (and would be perceived as) the final rejection of the once powerful queen. The symbolic implication of the marriage was that her services were no longer needed to ensure peace at the borders of the Macedonian kingdom.

In celebration of this marriage a great festival was arranged. Alexander was present at the festivities (some form of reconciliation had taken place) that would bind his sister to his uncle. As Philip, the gracious host, entered the theatre where the opening ceremony was about to be held, he was stabbed in the heart by Pausanias, the captain of his bodyguard. A young Macedonian noble, Pausanias had a bitter grievance against the new queen's uncle Attalus and against Philip for denying him justice concerning a lover's quarrel. A number of their contemporaries, however, suspected foul play, speculating that Olympias and/or Alexander had played some part in Philip's death. They generally assumed that Olympias had incited the bodyguard to do the deed, because she (and Alexander) had the most to gain from Philip's death. The truth will never be known, however.

A new king

After his father's murder in 336 BC Alexander became King Alexander III. Given the suspicious nature of Philip's death, however, Alexander found himself surrounded by enemies at home and threatened by rebellion abroad. To put his house in order, the first thing he did was to dispose speedily of all conspirators and domestic enemies, some of them alleged to be behind the murder. He also quickly executed several rival claimants to the throne, including his cousin Amyntas, whose throne Philip had usurped. He spared the life of his retarded half-brother, Arridaeus, however.

In consolidating his position, Alexander was helped by two of the more senior statesmen who had served under his father. The men would continue working with Alexander for years: Antipater eventually became his regent in Greece and Macedonia, and

Parmenion (having secured a foothold in Asia Minor during Philip's lifetime) became his second in command and would be his most important general during the earlier part of his campaigns.

Olympias also rid herself of enemies, with extreme ferocity. The second child of Eurydice, Philip's young bride, had been a son, and Olympias is said to have had both children killed in the mother's presence before forcing the unhappy woman to hang herself.

Not only were there internal threats to be dealt with as Alexander assumed the throne; external threats to the new king were also formidable. The leaders of the Greek city-states saw Philip's murder as a godsend, an opportunity to rid themselves of Macedonian interference in their affairs. They expected that the king's young successor would be a pushover. That assumption proved to be terribly wrong, however. Alexander quickly showed his talent as an incisive strategist and brilliant tactician by putting down uprisings in Thrace and Illyria. His next problem was Thebes, which had revolted on the false rumour that Alexander was dead. The Thebans voted to join forces with Athens and Persia to over-throw what they saw as the Macedonian "dictatorship". Furious that these states had accused him of being a dictator, Alexander rushed south, marching his tired army an astonishing 400 kilo-metres in thirteen days, razed Thebes, and sold the inhabitants off as slaves. It was his dramatic way of demonstrating that he would not tolerate any transgression against his authority. Because he saw himself as the champion of all Greece, he decided to spare Athens, however, not wanting to be viewed as a despot in the city that had been the birthplace of democracy.

Cowed by the severity of his action against Thebes, the grum-bling Greek city-states fell into line. In Athens the leading statesmen and philosophers came to congratulate Alexander for his success in assuming leadership in Greece. One famous character, however, is said to have been conspicuous by his absence from that group: Diogenes. Curious to meet the philosopher, Alexander went to that part of the city where Diogenes lived. He found the man naked except for a loincloth, sunning himself. Diogenes, disturbed by the noise of Alexander's arrival, looked at the imposing leader but said nothing. Finally, in desperation Alexander asked him if there was anything he wanted. Diogenes, replying in a now-famous affirma-tive, nodded and asked him to step aside as he was standing in his

*Alexander listening to The Oracle of Delphi. "Romance of Alexander":
Armenian manuscript, fourteenth century, Venice*

sun. Although the new king's numerous courtiers made fun of the
matter, Alexander is said to have replied enigmatically, "If I were
not Alexander, I would be Diogenes" (Plutarch, 1973, p. 266).

With his own house in order (though not to the satisfaction of
Antipater and Parmenion, who had advised him to establish a line

of succession), Alexander was now ready for the Persian campaign. Because he had an unshakeable faith in the predictive power (and reliability) of oracles, he visited Delphi to consult the oracle before starting his expedition. Arriving at a time the oracle could not be consulted, Alexander—impatient as always—refused to wait. The priestess, exasperated at being forced to give in to his demands, declared, "You are invincible, my son" (Plutarch, 1973, p. 266).

Alexander interpreted this statement as an omen of his future success. Having inherited from his father the most perfectly organized, trained, and equipped fighting machine of antiquity, he was now prepared to conquer the world.

CHAPTER FOUR

A strategic genius

A lexander, like his father, was obsessed by the idea of leading an expedition into Asia. The "party line" reason that he handed out for popular consumption was that the campaign was necessary to redress the insult of the Persian invasion by the great king Xerxes 150 years earlier; the Greek cities of Asia Minor needed to be liberated. But there were other reasons, less worthy and therefore less touted. For example, Alexander badly needed the Persian wealth to maintain the costly army built up by his father. In spite of the rich mineral resources of Macedonia, Alexander incurred great debts maintaining the formidable army. (Alexander, like Philip, was a lavish spender, especially when it came to military might, and the financial strain on the Macedonian kingdom had been tremendous.) In addition, a less rational reason for the expedition was that Alexander wanted not only to complete, but particularly to surpass, what his father had started.

Alexander started his march with an allied Greek army that proved to be one of the most impressive in history. Initially, the number of troops was unimpressive in comparison with the forces of the Persian king. The numbers increased, however, as Alexander carried out his remarkable campaign. As he continued his march into Asia, his troops were augmented mightily, primarily due to the recruitment of mercenaries from Greece and elsewhere who joined him as the campaign progressed. (Later, after his conquest of Persia, he would also train 30,000 young Persians for three years in Macedonian ways of war. These Persians would be integrated into Macedonian units, and eventually the army in Asia would consist predominantly of Persian troops.)

Conqueror of Asia

In the spring of 334 BC Alexander crossed the Hellespont (now the Dardanelles) heading for Asia, leaving Antipater, the general and old friend of his father, as his deputy in Europe. Alexander commanded about 30,000 foot soldiers and over 5,000 cavalry, of whom nearly 14,000 were Macedonians and about 7,000 were allies of the Greek league. This army had an excellent mixture of weapons: there were lightly armed Cretan and Macedonian archers, warriors from Thracia, and Agrianian javelin men (who, like modern-day Ghurkas, were able mountaineers). The striking force was the cavalry, though the core of the army was the infantry phalanx (9,000 strong) and Royal Shield-bearers (3,000 men strong). Pride of place among the mounted troops was held by the Macedonian Companion Cavalry, a force that included the "Royal Squadron", Alexander's own bodyguard, which would spearhead the devastating cavalry charges in the major battles. Along with the army Alexander took engineers, surveyors, architects, scientists, court officials, and even historians (Dupuy, 1969). Because he viewed his campaigns in part as scientific expeditions, he had his scientists and surveyors send records and specimens of animal and plant life to Aristotle on a regular basis.

According to some sources, Alexander would not start his expedition without assuring the welfare of all his companions. Before departure he is assumed to have signed away most of the property of the crown. One of his Companions, Perdiccas, is supposed to have asked him, "But your majesty, what are you leaving for yourself?" The reply was "my hopes" (Plutarch, p. 267).

The story goes that when the army reached land after crossing the Dardanelles, Alexander leaped from his ship in full armour and,

Persian soldiers: relief, Persepolis

hurling his spear ahead, declared, "I accept Asia from the gods" (Arrian, 1971; Diodorus, 1992, 17.17.2). With this statement he announced his intention to retain his conquests as royal territory and began his war on Persia—a war that his father had been planning for years.

The Persian kingdom of that day was an empire of epic proportions, stretching from Egypt and the Mediterranean into India and central Asia. It had dominated the ancient world for over two centuries. Alexander's main opponent there was King Darius III, the last in the line of the so-called Great Kings of Persia, an empire started with Cyrus the Great (who ruled from 548 to 529 BC). Because King Darius commanded incredibly huge armies, he would be a worthy opponent for the young warrior.

Alexander defeated Darius during three major engagements. The first encounter came in 334 BC, when Alexander swept away a Persian defence force sent (but not headed) by King Darius at the Granicus River (located in present-day Turkey). This defence force was not the "royal" army; it was an assembly of troops under the command of the satraps of the region. The Rhodian mercenary general Memnon, their foremost commander, had advocated a "scorched earth" strategy against Alexander's invasion, rather than

"The Battle of Issus": *Roman mosaic from Greek painting, Pompeii*

an open battle. However, several of the Persian satraps, hesitant to lay waste to their realms, apparently rejected his approach. According to most students of the battle, the main cause of Persian failure at the Granicus was the lack of consensus among Persian commanders; they had no cohesive battle plan. Furthermore, many of the Persian generals took a relaxed view towards the invading force, viewing Alexander as a young upstart. They saw him as an inexperienced, unproven entity and expected him to be a pushover.

A major by-product of Alexander's victory at the Granicus was that many prominent Persian commanders were killed. His later rapid advance through almost the whole of Asia Minor—not slowed until the Battle of Issus—was facilitated by the fact that there were hardly any Persian satraps remaining who were talented enough to organize a proper resistance. The battle was a great morale booster as well. Alexander's army, in its first successful campaign in Persian territory, had demonstrated the weaknesses of the Persian Empire. Numbers alone could not vanquish incisive strategy, great training, rigorous discipline, and speed of action. Despite the Persian army's enormous advantage in numbers, the encounter had shown that the Persian force was sluggish; it lacked the speed and adaptability of the well-oiled Macedonian fighting machine. Alexander had discovered that with the help of the Companion Cavalry and the phalanx, he could expect to be victorious over any Persian army (Fuller, 1989; Keegan, 1988).

King Darius at the battle of Issus: detail of mosaic, Pompeii

Having taken most of Asia Minor expeditiously, Alexander entered Northern Syria. In 333 BC Darius faced the invader in person near the town of Issus (in today's southern Turkey). The Greek army was outnumbered many times (perhaps by as much as ten to one). Alexander's network of informers had apprised him of the inexperience of some of the troops in the battle formation of

Darius, however, so the Greek king rushed his Companion Cavalry towards those inexperienced troops who could not stand up to the Macedonian assault. The missile javelins of the Persians were no match for the stabbing spears of the Macedonians. As these weaker units were routed, they opened the way for Alexander to push his attack towards the centre, where King Darius was positioned. Alexander's speed in attacking did not give the Persian commanders time to reorganize. Darius's courage failed him as the phalanx trampled ever closer down the line. In panic, he turned his chariot and fled, a scene well captured in the Issus mosaic from the House of the Faun in Pompeii, now in the National Museum in Naples. With the retreat of Darius, the whole Persian army disintegrated. Military strategists still marvel at how Alexander turned great odds into an overwhelming victory at the Battle of Issus.

King Darius had been so confident of success that he had brought his family with him to Issus. The speed and surprise of the Greek victory enabled Alexander to capture the entire Persian royal household—Darius's mother (Sisygambis), his wife, and his children. After the battle, when the victor entered Darius's tent in all its luxury—with its golden bath, silk carpets, and so on—Alexander (who was known for living in spartan conditions) is reported to have commented, "So this, it seems, is what it is to be a king" (Plutarch, 1973, p. 275).

Alexander treated the captured royal household with great respect, a well-thought-out political manoeuvre that served him well, as the queen mother was a powerful figure in Persian dynastic politics. He also gave instructions that the royals were to receive an education in Greek language and customs. This teaching of the customs of the conquerors was a prelude of things to come, the beginning of Hellenization. Alexander, meanwhile, took over Darius's role, trying to use the latter's family to establish his own legitimacy as king of Asia.

Moving onward, Alexander met serious resistance at Tyre (just off the coast of present-day Lebanon), a strongly fortified island. Arriving at the island fortress, Alexander demanded that the sequestered Tyrians make a sacrifice to the god Melquart, whom he equated with his assumed ancestor Heracles. The city refused, a denial that would be deeply regretted by the inhabitants of the city. Alexander was in a rage over the city's defiance, but even if he had wanted to ignore the resistance and move onward he could not have, because he feared the possibility of an attack to his rear.

The siege of Tyre proved to be one of the most difficult military operations of Alexander's entire career. Given the city's offshore location, Alexander decided to build a land bridge, a construction that still exists. After a seven-month siege, he finally gained entry via a brutal naval battle. The storming of Tyre in July 332 BC was one of Alexander's greatest military achievements. It was followed by a great massacre (the crucifixion of 2,000 Tyrian fighters along the seashore) and the sale of the women and children into slavery. The reasons for this brutal ending were many: Alexander's initial rage at not being able to make sacrifices to his supposed ancestor Heracles, his frustration over the long siege, and the murder of a number of Macedonian envoys sent to offer peace in return for surrender before the start of the siege.

During the siege of Tyre, Darius sent a letter to Alexander with an offer to end the conflict: he offered to pay a ransom of 10,000 talents for his family and was prepared to cede all his lands west of the Euphrates. Alexander's principal general, Parmenion, advised him to accept the offer. "I would accept, were I Alexander," Parmenion said. "That is what I should do were I Parmenion" (Arrian, 1971, p. 144) was Alexander's famous retort.

Moving on from Tyre, Alexander continued conquering what was left of the Persian Empire. He captured Gaza next and then passed on into Egypt. The Persian satrap in that territory wisely surrendered. The people greeted Alexander as a deliverer, because the Egyptians hated their Persian rulers for failing to pay proper respect to Egyptian religious practices. At Memphis Alexander sacrificed to Apis (the Greek name for Hapi, the sacred Egyptian bull) and was crowned with the traditional double crown of the pharaohs; the native priests were placated and their religion encouraged. By these successes Alexander secured control of the entire eastern Mediterranean coastline. To solidify his victory, he founded the Egyptian city of Alexandria on a strip of land between Lake Mareotis and the Mediterranean Sea—a city that would soon become a world centre of commerce and learning.

Turning northward again, Alexander reorganized his forces at Tyre and started for Babylon with an army of 40,000 infantry and 7000 cavalry. Crossing the Euphrates and the Tigris Rivers, he met

Alexander portrayed as the Egyptian pharaoh: monumental statue, Luxor

Darius at the head of an army of unknown size. (Although we have no exact figures, the accounts of antiquity—probably exaggerated—claim that it numbered a million men.) He completely defeated this army in the Battle of Gaugamela, in present-day Iraq. Alexander's brilliant victory at this battle in 331 BC (based on a battle plan still discussed at length at military academies) irrevocably changed the course of history. Darius fled as he had done at Issus and, to the great disappointment of Alexander (who probably wanted to use him as a local ruler under his authority) was soon killed by one of his generals, an act of regicide that granted Alexander his goal of being king of Asia.

Babylon surrendered after the Battle of Gaugamela. As in Egypt, the local priesthood was encouraged to continue worshipping their gods. The city of Susa, with its enormous treasures, soon followed. Then, in midwinter, Alexander forced his way to Persepolis, the Persian capital. After plundering the royal treasury and taking other rich booty, Alexander decided to sack the city itself after a suggestion made by a courtesan at a drunken party (if legend is to be believed). The real reason for the destruction of the city may have been retribution for Persian acts of sacrilege against the Greek gods during earlier conquests in Greece. Another possible reason may have been the Persians' reluctance to welcome him (a man unused to opposition) as the new ruler. Some scholars of Alexander, however, view the incident as the result of an impulsive decision to pay off the Greek troops, because the material rewards had thus far been relatively meagre (looting and plundering being usually forbidden) (Bosworth, 1988). Whatever the reason (or, more probably, *reasons*), the city and its palace were reduced to rubble. With that devastation, Alexander completed the destruction of the ancient Persian Empire. He gave specific orders, however, to leave the monuments, particularly the tomb of Cyrus the Great, a king he greatly admired, intact. He also made it a point to visit this tomb.

Alexander's domain now extended along and beyond the southern shores of the Caspian Sea (including modern Afghanistan and Baluchistan) and northward into Bactria and Sogdiana (modern Western Turkistan, also known as Central Asia). It had taken Alexander only three years—from the spring of 334 BC to the spring of 331 BC—to master this vast area.

The capitals of Persia were now in Alexander's hands, and he had gained possession of the vast gold reserves of the former "Great Kings". But having gained this empire was not enough for him. Alexander and his army marched ever further eastward, battling nomadic warriors and rebels on what were considered the northeastern fringes of the known world. In order to complete his conquest of the remnants of the Persian Empire, which had once included part of western India, Alexander eventually crossed the Indus River in 326 BC and entered the region bordering the Persian province of Taxila. Here he met the feared Indian monarch Porus, who, with 25,000 men and 200 elephants (one of the highest numbers of these behemoths ever employed in any battle of Western classical history), nearly managed to do what the entire Persian Empire had not been able to accomplish. But then Porus had a competitive advantage: horses are scared of elephants, so his multitude of pachyderms rendered the Macedonian cavalry all but useless.

For about two weeks Alexander moved his troops up and down the western bank of the river Hydapes, pretending to make the crossing into Taxila. Porus followed suit, shadowing his movements until he became tired of all the false alarms and let down his guard. When Porus had finally been lulled into complacency, Alexander crossed the river during the night, taking him by surprise. Even modern logistic experts admire the ability of the Macedonians to transport an entire fighting force across a swollen Indian monsoon river in just a single night. King Porus surrendered and became a reliable ally.

As in the case of Porus, Alexander would respect and pardon a brave enemy. He always made sure that collaboration was presented as a much more attractive proposition than resistance. Most often, capitulation of an enemy force was rewarded with kindness; revolts, however, were suppressed ruthlessly. It was a well-calculated strategy designed to minimize battlefield losses. Adversaries were more inclined to submit to Alexander knowing that they would be pardoned and included in his empire (and realizing that the alternative was extremely unattractive).

During his campaigns, Alexander loved to tackle apparently impossible challenges, be they unbeaten adversaries or seemingly

War elephant: terracotta, Louvre museum

impregnable rock fortresses. He would be the first to attack the Theban Sacred Band, mount an imposing city wall, or climb an impregnable rock. One famous obstacle he encountered on his journeys was the Rock of Aornus, a natural formation rising almost three thousand metres above the Indus River. The demi-god Heracles was said to have failed to take this rock as he wandered the earth performing his great labours. Working night and day, pushing tons of earth into a ravine, Alexander's troops eventually managed to create a causeway to get up the rock. As had happened on many other occasions, Alexander was the first on the rock to face the defenders, defying Heracles to be the greatest besieger in history.

A reflective practitioner

As a field commander Alexander was among the greatest that history has ever seen. Loved by his troops, he maintained meticulous discipline none the less. He was a brilliant strategist, willing to adopt new tactics and create innovative forms of warfare, perfecting the military innovations started by his father and devising new ones of his own (as illustrated in his ability to improvise and adopt guerilla tactics, fighting tribal groups in Afghanistan and against King Porus and his elephants in India). Although frequently outnumbered, he used surprise, improvisation, and the lie of the land to extract himself from the most impossible situations. He always made it a point to know the battlefield better than his opponents, and he then used that military reconnaissance to maximum advantage. He was a master at confusing the enemy regarding his intentions, he used decisiveness and speed as effective weapons, he created and maintained good lines of communication, and he encouraged his engineering corps to think creatively, resulting in battering rams, catapults, ladders, bridges, and siege towers that allowed the Macedonians to breach the most impregnable of strongholds.

Alexander was also a brilliant tactician, able to grasp the enemy's unspoken intentions and adapt and improvise accordingly. He had an uncanny talent for quickly determining the weak spots in the enemy line; and when there was none, he knew how to lure his adversaries away from optimal battle conditions. In addition to putting his opponents at a disadvantage, he often managed to get them to respond in ways that he desired. Using these psychological tools to his advantage, he was able to coordinate all the elements of his war machine in lightning-quick, devastating attacks.

Alexander was at his best in battle situations. No matter how grim the circumstances, he kept his cool, never panicking. He always executed his plans in a coherent and coordinated manner, sifting deftly through conflicting reports and making correct judgments, however stressful the battle conditions. He showed unusual versatility in his use of both weaponry and tactics, adapting both as needed. He was extremely successful at all the types of armed confrontation that he undertook: more traditional warfare, sieges, anti-guerrilla actions, and ambushes. It is this global mastery of warfare, in combination with tactical and strategic skill, which makes him unique. Under his leadership, his men never lost a battle—not once!—and their losses on the field were relatively few compared to those of their adversaries.

CHAPTER FIVE

Administering an empire

The Persians had made it a habit to absorb, after conquest, the individual countries they had vanquished, leaving their internal structures largely intact. The old institutions were coordinated in the name of the king by a Persian satrap on whose behalf taxes were collected, and the local bureaucrats who had been running those institutions were retained, maximizing Persian administrative efficiency. It was the custom of the Great Kings to appoint members of their family and entourage as satraps. The reigning king was thus informed of the happenings in his empire by his agents, known as the "king's eyes".

Alexander admired the Persian way of administering an empire, as reflected in what he saw in his travels and what he read of the administration of Cyrus the Great. He also learned a lot about governance from the contributions of Aristotle. He knew that to understand and, when necessary, manipulate another society, he needed to identify the true centres of power, as well as their linkages, loyalties, and pressure points. He recognized that tribal and religious leaders would usually hold the main positions of power, and he saw the advantages of using the experience of these constituencies by supporting them. Furthermore, he knew that treating the subjugated people fairly would be the easiest method to get their support in return—support that he sorely needed, since he had only a small number of Macedonian citizen troops with him that could be used for controlling the empire.

To make this philosophy work, Alexander made very clear the advantages of collaboration. As a liberator, he strove to be sensitive to the local culture, treating with respect and tact any kings or tribal chiefs who pledged alliance to his ever-growing empire. If such leaders were prepared to collaborate, he would allow them to administer on his behalf. For example, when Alexander conquered Egypt, he upheld all traditional practices, also restoring and rebuilding Egypt's religious centres (heeding Aristotle's comments about keeping the local priests on one's side). Alexander was an advocate of Greek syncretism, seeing the deities of Asia as local manifestations of the Greek gods. He had no interest in imposing other gods upon them. By showing respect for the local traditions—something the Persians had *not* done—he increased the likelihood that he would be hailed as a saviour and liberator. Those people who opposed his rule, however, often experienced his terrible wrath—Thebes and Tyre being bloody examples.

In many of the Greek towns of Asia Minor that surrendered and were freed from Persian rule, Alexander exempted the inhabitants from tribute payments to the Great King and left local laws intact. He also generally placed a ban on looting and plundering, thereby winning local support. As self-declared king of Asia, the land was his possession, and the people his subjects. Given this position of ownership, encouraging destruction and enslaving his new subjects would have been a self-defeating proposition. As a result of Alexander's cooperative approach, for most of the people of Asia Minor not very much changed. Macedonians replaced the Persian satraps, the tribute was now called a *contribution*, and ultimate authority resided not with the Great King but with the new great king, Alexander.

Alexander's administrative talents were evident not only in his establishment of Macedonian rule in Persia, but also in his organization of the supply train for his troops. Because he had banned plundering, his army could not live off the land, as some armies did; it needed to be supplied on a constant basis. Feeding and equipping the number of people and animals needed to keep his large army functioning must have been a logistical nightmare, particularly given the time period he was living in. And yet he ran the supply train so effectively that his army continued to operate at lightning speed even far from home.

Creating a melting pot

Following Aristotle's advice that a king must balance power between different parties, Alexander began to use a combination of locals, Persians, and Macedonians to rule his growing empire, though he filled key administrative positions with Greeks. He made different officers responsible for military, financial, and civil duties, spreading the responsibility broadly. He centralized his financial policy by using collectors independent of the local governors and had all revenues sent to his finance officer, bypassing intermediate administrators. Although this reduced graft considerably, exploitation seemed to be permissible as long as sufficient revenue was generated for the government.

Alexander set up garrisons all over his empire, each typically placed under the command of a Companion. He left each leader with a large number of garrison troops to deal with eventual resistance to his rule. Usually, these garrisons were also the foundations of new cities. Alexander has been unsurpassed as the founder of cities, with more than seventy credited to his name. And he did not leave them to founder or flourish on their own: he made a major effort to populate his new cities by transplanting Greek and Macedonian settlers.

Another of Alexander's innovations was to train young men from the conquered territories for service in his army. He required prospective soldiers to learn Greek and be trained in Macedonian weaponry, offering what might be called the first state-supported system of education to the best and the brightest among his young Asian subjects. With these efforts, Alexander laid the foundation for what has been called "Hellenization".

As he stabilized his growing empire, one of Alexander's major problems was where to establish his base of rule. Would it remain at Pella in Macedonia, as the old guard hoped, or would it shift to a moving court in Asia? Although initially he operated from both centres, power's centre of gravity gradually favoured Asia, where

Alexander hoped to strengthen his base of power. To the great concern of his Macedonian inner circle, he started to create partnerships with Asians, no longer limiting senior positions to Macedonians. Not only the governance but also the court itself was changing: the moving court in Asia was taking on the pomp and ambience of a traditional Persian court, in contrast to the more low-key court in Pella. To add insult to injury, Alexander didn't seem to mind the obsequious behaviour of his Persian subjects nor their constant praise for his many achievements. In other words, Alexander was making a distinction in form between his role as king of Asia and his role as king of Macedonia.

Alexander understood the importance of coinage in international transactions. He founded a number of royal mints throughout the empire to facilitate trade, feeding them with the gold reserves of the Persian kings. He established a new coinage under his name, helping to improve trade throughout his empire and allowing him to pay his enormous army and finance the building of new cities and ports.

Some historians have presented Alexander as a visionary who believed in the peaceful coexistence of different nations and races within his empire. They refer, for example, to the mass weddings ordered by Alexander to bring together Greeks and Persians. (Eighty of Alexander's most important men were required to marry highborn Persian women in traditional Persian wedding ceremonies, and he set the example by himself marrying the late King Darius's daughter and another Persian princess, having earlier also married the daughter of a Bactrian leader.)

In general, though, the coexistence was anything but peaceful. As the months and years went by, the so-called pro-Persian policy created increasing friction in Alexander's relations with the rest of the Macedonians, who had no understanding of (and no appreciation for) his new conception of the empire. His determination to incorporate Persians on equal terms into the administration of the provinces, into the cavalry bodyguard, and into the army—as noted earlier, he provided Macedonian military training to 30,000 Persian young men—was heavily criticized by many Macedonians. They resented his integration policies, looked down on those members of the aristocracy who had been admitted to the bodyguard, and referred to the Persian soldiers sarcastically as "war dancers".

Marriage of Alexander and Darius' daughter Barsine in 324 BC:
fresco from Pompeii

The drive to move on

Alexander, though rich in talents and strengths, had one notable
weakness: he was unable to consolidate his empire. Running a
stable state was not for him. He was driven to go on, to make further
conquests. He simply could not stop. He refused to make peace
with Darius, for example (as we saw earlier), even though his most
senior general, Parmenion, advised him to accept the Persian king's

favourable offer during the siege of Tyre. Parmenion, advising consolidation over further conquest, felt that the risks of further campaigning were extraordinarily high, especially given that a large part of the newly conquered territory remained unsettled and un-unified.

Because there was no effective supervision of his officials, corruption and oppression gradually took root and eventually became widespread. Although Alexander's conviction that conquered populations should be involved in their own governance was a relatively new concept, he had not pushed innovation further and built creative structures of government. The prosaic details of long-term administration bored him. Taking the short-term view, he simply replaced one loosely structured empire with another, without putting into place the mechanisms that would have allowed it to last. Furthermore, although he took sufficient interest in his newly founded cities to populate them with outsiders, he made no real effort to integrate the settlers into the local community. As a result, the original population often saw the new people as costly intruders. The settlers, for their part, were reluctant colonists, often staying in Persia only because of fear of Alexander. Many of them longed to return to the Greek way of life.

CHAPTER SIX

Striving for the "Endless Ocean"

Alexander's empire now stretched from the Balkans down to Nubia and across the Punjab. But having conquered part of India was still not enough for the adventurous Alexander. He wanted to reach the "Endless Ocean", that vast expanse of water that the Greeks believed formed the edge of the known world. To go to the actual boundary of the world (which was thought to lie beyond India) was an irresistible challenge. Alexander had derived his geographical understanding from the teachings of Aristotle, who thought that India was a small peninsula running into a vast sea. As Alexander saw it, he could push on to the Ganges River and continue to the shores of the Endless Ocean. He was determined to march to the very ends of the earth. Once he succeeded in finalizing this conquest, the kingdom of Asia would be bounded by desert and by the waters of the great sea—a practical result, given that the gained territories, with their difficult borders, would be more easily defended against enemies. But apart from this pragmatic reason for further conquest, Alexander's love of adventure, his thirst for knowledge, and his curiosity for the unknown drove him ever forward.

In 326 bc, having marched across a broad expanse of India, Alexander and his men arrived at the rain-swollen Beas River close

Alexander the Great: Moghul miniature

to Lahore, a destination that would be the turning point, both for the campaign and for Alexander (Bosworth, 1988; Kazantzakis, 1982). In his fervour to reach the Endless Ocean, he had miscalculated the mood of his men. Morale had been dropping steadily, and he had not observed its plunge. After eight years of fighting in searing heat, freezing snow, and incessant monsoon rains, the troops were desperate to leave the horrors of the present Indian campaign behind and embark on the long march home. The youthful soldiers who had eagerly crossed the Hellespont with Alexander almost a decade earlier were now cynical, battle-hardened veterans. Very few of them had gone through the travails unscathed. All were exhausted; many were sick. With their equipment in disarray as well, they were close to the breaking point. More money, or the permission to engage in plundering, no longer had much motivating effect. Furthermore, the soldiers felt a growing antagonism against Alexander's adoption of Persian ways; they did not share his vision of the equality of people of all cultures and therefore did not approve of forced intermarriages with Persian women. They were also confused about the two roles he was playing: a Macedonian king who had simple habits, and the Great King of Asia, a grotesque example of luxury and extravagance (Green, 1991; Hammond, 1998).

Facing this dangerous crossing so soon after the difficult victory against King Porus (and his elephants), Alexander found his charisma failing him for the first time. Despite a dramatic speech exhorting his soldiers to continue their glorious exploits, he was unable to win over the reluctant majority. One of his main commanders, General Coenus, bravely spoke out: "There is one thing above all others a successful man should know," he said; "it is when to stop" (Arrian, 1971, p. 297). Loud cheers from the other soldiers supported this statement. Alexander, extremely upset by both the comment and the men's response, tried to shame his soldiers, telling them that they were deserting their king in the middle of enemy territory and that he would go on without them. Then he retreated, like Achilles, to his tent, nursing his wrath, trying to overcome his depressive thoughts, and hoping that his officers would have a change of heart. But the men stuck to their position, and after three days Alexander realized that he was backed into a corner. Hanging on to his position could lead to an insurrection of the troops. Cunning as always, he made a sacrifice concerning the crossing of the swollen river and then reported that his diviners saw the omens for continuation as unfavourable, thereby avoiding a confrontation. Shortly thereafter he gave the order to turn back.

So as not to lose face, Alexander held a celebration of that momentous decision. He organized equestrian and athletic games

Alexander pleading with his officers by the river Beas. "The Romance of Alexander": Armenian manuscript, fourteenth century, Venice

and ordered the construction of twelve gigantic altars on the banks of the Beas River to mark the eastern limit of his empire. A brass obelisk inscribed with the simple words "Alexander stopped here" was also erected at the site. Alexander knew, however, that the land just beyond the Ganges River would have been an easy conquest, because a weak, unpopular king ruled it. He would never quite be able to forgive his men for their refusal to continue.

Trying to make the best of a frustrating situation, Alexander decided to "retreat" via a route that would allow him to conquer all of southern India. He constructed a fleet and passed down the Indus to reach its mouth (where Karachi is now located) in September 325 BC The fleet then crossed the Persian Gulf, and Alexander and his army returned over land. It was an excruciating march through the desert regions of modern Baluchistan, southern Afghanistan, and southern Iran, with shortages of food and water (due to the failure of a scheduled supply convoy that was unable to reach them) causing severe hardship and many deaths among his troops. Alexander suffered with them, showing his solidarity: when his men ran out of horses—it was a rugged journey for beasts as well—Alexander dismounted and walked in front of his troops; when given some water, he poured it on the sand to show that he would drink only when all others could drink (though he must have been suffering considerably from an unhealed wound) (Arrian, 1971).

When he decided to send home those Macedonian troops no longer fit for service, another rebellion occurred, this time by those who felt that they were being discarded in favour of the young Persian "ballet" soldiers. In their irritation at what they saw as a lack of consideration for their services, some made fun of Alexander, ridiculing his new recruits and his proclaimed ancestry to Zeus-Ammon. Not any longer used to such frank interchanges, the king flew into a rage and berated the men for their ingratitude, reminding them that (as he saw it) he had transformed them from impoverished vagabonds to citizens of the greatest state in the Aegean. Then he stormed off and went into seclusion for a few days, nursing his depression. Afterwards he began to transfer Macedonian military titles to Persian units and surrounded himself exclusively with Persian staff. The Macedonians, properly subdued, asked forgiveness for their remarks and actions and offered the surrender of the instigators of the mutiny. Alexander decided to be magnanimous, and considerable rejoicing followed.

Soon thereafter, in 324 BC, Alexander's dearest friend, Hephaestion, died of a high fever in the city of Susa (in what is now Iran).

The two had been inseparable companions for years, having shared their education under Aristotle. The king, grief-stricken, sheared off his hair in a gesture of mourning and ordered that the manes and tails of all the horses and mules also be cut. To honour his friend, he arranged a funeral whose magnificence has rarely been equalled. After a period of mourning, he sought to numb his grief through action, undertaking a forty-day campaign against a local tribe that had not taken well to subjugation.

Alexander then spent about a year organizing his dominions and completing a survey of the Persian Gulf in preparation for consolidation of his conquests in the Arab peninsula. He arrived in Babylon, in the heart of the former Persian Empire, in the spring of 323 BC Those who had returned safely with Alexander to the site of their earlier conquests had covered over 20,000 miles within a period of roughly ten years!

After his arrival in Babylon Alexander immersed himself in a range of ambitious projects, the most important being a campaign against Arabia as he had received no acknowledgement of his rule from this former ally of king Darius. He envisioned combining Asia and Europe into one country, with Babylon as the new capital. In order to attain this goal, he had corrupt officials executed and then worked more diligently than ever to spread Greek ideas, customs, and laws into Asia. Alexander again began promoting Persians to high-ranking positions in his army, arguing that Persians and Macedonians should share the empire (in keeping with his earlier decision to push for marriages that united the two empires).

Alexander decided to prepare a huge naval force to start an Arabian campaign to consolidate his gains around the Persian Gulf. As he planned a voyage by sea to settle the coast of the Persian Gulf, he received a number of bad omens. In spite of these omens, however, he continued preparing for the new expedition. By May he was sick with a fever that kept him in bed. Whether it was caused by an infection, malaria (or some other tropical disease), or poisoning at the hands of senior officers worried about his inability to stop his conquests, we will never know. Despite Alexander's extraordinarily strong constitution, the fever had a dangerously debilitating effect on his battle-ravaged body. One of the Macedonian officers sitting at his bedside asked him to whom he would leave his empire. *"Hoti to kratisto"* ("To the best"), he whispered. Others later argued that he had said, "To the *strongest*". Still others, noting that the words *"kratisto"* and *"kratero"* sound quite alike, thought that he referred to Craterus, the general then highest in Alexander's trust (Arrian, 1971, p. 394).

Soldiers lamenting Alexander's death. "The Romance of Alexander":
Armenian manuscript, fourteenth century, Venice

Shortly thereafter, on 10 June 323 BC, Alexander the Great died. He was only thirty-two years old. Although his first wife, Roxane, was pregnant with his first child at the time of the king's death, he left no heir: Roxane and mother Olympias were killed. The king's direct line had become extinct. After his death the empire he had worked so passionately to create fell into anarchistic chaos, a bloody struggle between his surviving commanders that no one man won.

In spite of this chaotic ending to his reign, Alexander's legacy remains remarkably alive, even today. His explorations and conquests continue to speak to humankind's imagination (Hammond, 1998), recounted in the legends of Europe, Africa, and Asia. In Persia Alexander is known as Sikander, the "Two-Horned" one (because he liked to wear the ram's horns of Ammon when his portrait was painted). Afghan tribesmen and Greek fishermen alike still invoke him as an ancestral patron. For many people throughout the world, he is seen as a model of exemplary leadership.

And yet we have seen that Alexander had a dark side. Consider, for example, the 2,000 inhabitants of Tyre that he mercilessly crucified after the siege. Other power-based atrocities included the torture and killing of some of his own most loyal aides after the final defeat of King Darius, when his court was plagued by controversy and intrigue, and the brutal subjugation of the conquered peoples of India (when tempers were high and enthusiasm for adventure low). The justification for these acts is subject to debate to this day. In modern Iran Alexander is still seen as an evil king—a personification of the devil, in fact—who did his best to destroy the respectable old Persian culture and religion and who put Persepolis to the torch. In Arab memory he is often equated with a bogeyman; he is an object of fear with whom mothers threaten unruly children.

But in spite of his darker side, Alexander managed to have a huge impact. How did he achieve his success? What steps did he take to create meaning for his people (and for those who came afterwards)? What made him such a special leader, and what lessons can he teach us about leadership?

PART II
LEADERSHIP

Alexander as the god Helios: terracotta medallion, first century BC

CHAPTER SEVEN

The management of meaning

An essential part of effective leadership is the management of meaning. Effective leaders speak to the collective imagination of their followers. They create a group identity by articulating and sharing their own dreams, painting vivid descriptions of a future state that touch the unconscious of their people (Freud, 1921; Kets de Vries, 2001a). They possess the uncanny ability to externalize their internal theatre and perform it on a public stage (Lasswell, 1960). They know how to tie in their personal vision with the historical moment (Erikson, 1958, 1963). They foster this process of meaning-management by using language, ceremonies, symbols, and setting.

Leadership and stagecraft, business and theatre, join forces as effective leaders use strategic manoeuvres to mobilize psychological support. Many strong leaders possess great oratorical skills and know how to make use of humour, irony, and the colloquial. Although they use simple language—the language of their audience—to talk directly to their followers' unconscious, they are adept at employing figurative language such as similes and metaphors to facilitate identification. Furthermore, they tap cultural roots, evoking (and emulating) historical and mythological figures, for example. All these devices, which effective leaders employ with an uncanny sense of timing (and even suspense!), are tools that allow their audience to understand what they have to say.

The unsettling emotional nature of the symbolic methods of communication used by effective (one might say "spellbinding") leaders induces the potentially dangerous reactions of dependency, regression, and transference (Freud, 1905; Kets de Vries, 1989). The psychological relationship between leaders and followers can, at times, be compared to that of hypnotists and their subjects. As leaders reawaken (through the compelling, authoritative nature of their message) past relationships of dominance and submission, they create in their followers a desire to be taken care of, inducing dependency reactions (Bion, 1959) that intertwine significant figures from childhood with contemporary figures. Past and present fuse in the person of the charismatic leader, and he or she becomes the depository of the followers' fantasies and hopes (Freud, 1921, 1929, 1930). In other words, followers "idealize" the leader.

Effective leaders realize (consciously or unconsciously) that the process of meaning-management requires painting the environment in sharp images, creating a Manichean world of light and darkness. Thus scapegoating—splitting the world into clear camps of us versus them, in-groups versus out-groups, or good versus bad—is an effective tool. It not only facilitates and intensifies group identification; it also allows followers to split off undesired (and undesirable) attributes and use others as depositories for those attributes. With the help of scapegoating (and the dramatization and histrionics that a simplified world of stark contrast demands), effective leaders can help transform and project followers' personal fears, aggressions, and aspirations on to social causes that allow for symbolic resolution. This regressive process of externalization results in a release of tension.

Clearly, the management of meaning is no simple task! Few people in history have mastered it as effectively as Alexander the Great did. His talent for speaking directly to the imagination of his troops, motivating and inspiring them, and his ability to use symbolic action to get his vision across was legendary. When Alexander set out on his Asian expedition, he made his initial intentions explicit: he declared himself the new ruler of Asia by throwing his spear in the soil of Asia after having crossed the Hellespont. He confirmed those intentions by stating (as he did often) that he was going to make right the wrongs done by the Xerxes, the Great King who had earlier invaded Greece. By articulating to his troops a sense of the righteousness of their cause, he earned their support.

Alexander had the "gift of grace" usually ascribed to prophets; his charisma was legendary. He had a special ability to transform ordinary labourers into extraordinary soldiers, to get the best out of his people, whatever their role. By dramatizing the risk—by telling his troops that they were up against impossible odds at the Battle of Issus, for example—and by reassuring them that they were none the less up to the challenge, he made them feel special. And his troops would accept the dare every time, rising to the occasion. Alexander knew how to "stretch" his men, creating in them a determined commitment that fuelled extraordinary effort.

Extremely creative, Alexander was always prepared to challenge the status quo. He possessed an uncanny talent to find new ways of dealing with complex situations. He knew how to use dialogue. By probing people in his inner circle he arrived at creative solutions. He was as imaginative in dealing with his adversaries as he was in dealing with his allies. He always sought new ways of looking at problems, whether those problems arose in battle situations or in more mundane encounters.

In addition to making his men feel valued, Alexander was good at emotionally touching and moving his people, demonstrating empathy through his actions. He possessed what has been called "the teddy bear factor"—the ability to make people feel comfortable (Kets de Vries, 2001a). He was a great "container" of others' emotions, putting his soldiers at ease. Furthermore, he conveyed the impression that he had all the time in the world for any soldier who wanted to address him (though, busy as he was, that had to have been an illusion); and when people talked to him, he really listened. He not only seemed to be, but *was*, a genuinely caring general.

Alexander's leadership style encouraged identification and group solidarity, in large part because he set the example of excellence. No armchair general or absentee commander, Alexander lived the life of his soldiers; he spoke their language. He suffered the same wounds as his troops, lived under canvas alongside them (at least until he became enamoured of Persian ways), and shared their food, their hardships, and their challenges. He was always ready for a drink or a game of dice with his men. Drinking parties with his Companions were opportunities for mutual praise singing—to reiterate heroic feats done in the past. During battle he could always be found at the front of his troops, easily recognizable by his white, two-plumed helmet. He led any attack in person and was usually the first man across a river, up and into a rock fortress, or over enemy lines. Unlike Darius, he never panicked under battle conditions. On the contrary, he kept an icy cool. Before each battle Alexander rode up and down the lines, singling out individuals and singing their praise to boost morale. He stopped before each unit to speak to his soldiers directly, calling out individuals and recounting their great deeds. He talked of the importance of each mission and assured the troops that their contributions would be recognized. After each battle he would again visit his men, examining their wounds, praising them for their valiant efforts, rewarding them handsomely for their success, and listening to their stories of valour. He also arranged extravagant ceremonial funerals for the fallen. During times of respite or peace, he provided recreational opportunities, arranging games and contests for the men. This excellent relationship with rank-and-file soldiers, characteristic from the start, was with Alexander almost to the end.

And it paid off. Affection for their leader galvanized his troops, inspiring them to march ever further and to excel at every endeavour. The unflagging determination of their king was often the only thing that kept them going when they faced seemingly impossible odds.

The manipulation of symbols

As we have seen, Alexander was no amateur in the motivation business. One of the earliest image marketers, he may have been the first conqueror to organize a publicity and propaganda department. During his campaigns, a day-to-day record was kept of Alexander's activities by Aristotle's nephew, Callisthenes, the expedition's official historian. This nephew made the most of his official dispatches,

using both faithful reporting and explanations of divine intervention when the latter suited Alexander's purposes. In that period of
history, divine signs were great motivational devices. The belief that
the gods were on one's side gave troops a real boost. A master at
applying symbolism, Alexander used priests and diviners to help
him when the situation required it, relying on his favourite diviner,
Aristander of Telmessus (who was with him throughout his time in
Asia), to advise him at critical moments.

One of Alexander's first acts on Asian soil was a visit to Troy,
where he offered sacrifices to Athena, the goddess of wisdom and
of battle, and to his supposed ancestor, Achilles. In doing so he
drew comparisons between the Greek's heroic past and the arduous
task that lay before him, casting himself in the role of Achilles.
When he reached Gordium (in present-day Turkey), he lost his
patience trying to untie the Gordian knot, and then, in a now-
famous incident, engaged in a public relations coup by untying the
knot by slashing through the rope with a sword. (The local oracle
had declared that he who untied the knot must rule over Asia.) In
332 BC, at the Egyptian oasis at Siwa (home of the renowned oracle
of the god Ammon), the priests allegedly confirmed that Alexander
had divine origins and that Ammon (who was often equated with
the Greeks' supreme deity Zeus, king of gods) was his true father.

The goddess Athena: gold coin from Sicyon, Greece, 323 BC

Alexander may have believed these pronouncements, but he most certainly encouraged reports of them for propaganda purposes. He used the priests' confirmation frequently, weaving their words (and the prophecies of the oracle and others) into his stories about future conquests. These divine associations surely helped to foster the many myths existing around his person (Fildes & Fletcher, 2001). When he heard that the tomb of Cyrus the Great had been desecrated, he lashed out in fury, and ordered it to be completely restored, viewing himself as the obvious descendant of this Great King. Desecration symbolized an attack on himself.

"Family romance" and the bid for divinity

Given Alexander's interest in his divine and heroic ancestors, it is interesting to reflect on the notion of the "family romance", the label that psychologists give to a fantasy often cherished by children having a difficult time reconciling conflict-ridden situations in the family (Fenichel, 1945). The family romance is a poetic tale in which the child pictures him- or herself as having been born of more distinguished parents and now being on a search for vindication and independence. It can also be seen as a way of denigrating a parent who is experienced as troublesome: finding the present parent lacking, the child fantasizes that the real, understanding parent must have been someone else, someone better.

The young Alexander, encouraged by his mother (particularly after the early family harmony was broken), fantasized that his earthly father was not really his father, that his true father was Zeus—a fantasy enriched by his identification with the semi-god Heracles and the mythological hero Achilles. Over time, however, Alexander seems to have taken his fantasy increasingly seriously. His mother's innuendos about his divine ancestry, combined with his experience with the Egyptian priests, all point in this direction. He increasingly felt that his achievements—which by now far outshone those of Heracles and Achilles in his own eyes—had earned him a place in the pantheon of gods. If he himself were seen as a god, that "promotion" would not only be a binding force in the empire he had created but would also help him surpass his father, who had had similar ambitions.

Alexander: divinely-inspired expression, Greek marble

Image-manipulation had a more visible side as well. For example, Alexander used his choice of dress as a propaganda tool, adopting native costumes wherever appropriate and wearing the purple robes and horned ram's head of Zeus-Ammon at banquets. Alexander also had a gift for manipulating his own portraiture for political ends. Throughout his reign he retained close control over his official image, whether sculpted, painted, or carved. In paintings or coins he was frequently portrayed with the horns of Zeus-Ammon; he was sometimes shown, like Heracles, wearing a helmet of lion skin; and on coins minted in Babylon he was depicted with Zeus's thunderbolt. His preferred sculptor, Lysippos, generally portrayed him in heroic poses. As these things show, self-deification became a major theme in Alexander's life, especially in the later years.

CHAPTER EIGHT

Entering the inner theatre of the king

W hen we try to evaluate Alexander, we have to remember that we are dealing with a personality that has been the inspiration of myths and legends for over twenty centuries. Alexander overshadowed the age in which he lived more than any man before or since. As we read stories about him—even stories written soon after his death—it is difficult to decide which statements are based on fact and which have been contaminated by the legends that began to form around his person even during his lifetime. Even a thorough study of this great conqueror is likely to yield a highly confused portrait, especially if it seeks to determine and depict the inner man.

An actor in search of a character

There is little agreement among scholars about the personality of Alexander. Since the time of his death in 323 BC, however, the various portrayals of the king have tended to cluster in three camps:

1. One school of thought views him as a murderous, predatory, narcissistic megalomaniac. Scholars who adhere to this opinion

are convinced that he was a brutal mercenary from Macedonia, out only to plunder the riches of the east—an autocrat who imposed his will by terror and violence. They suggest that he should be ranked in the annals of history with tyrants such as Stalin and Hitler.

2. Other scholars see Alexander as a charismatic, humanistic missionary determined to unify the races of the known world by creating a peacefully coexisting brotherhood of men and women built on cultural tolerance.

3. A third group takes an intermediate position. Adherents of this view perceive Alexander as an initially good and warm-hearted king, full of promise and noble intentions, who became a despotic tyrant after crossing into Persia and sampling the "fleshpots" and decadence of Babylon. Corrupted by "oriental" ways, weakened by over-indulgence in alcohol, and shadowed by depressive bouts, he became a paranoid megalomaniac who casually murdered good friends and wanted obsessively to be worshipped as a god.

Finding the real Alexander among these strikingly varied descriptions is difficult. And yet, although it is hard to find convergence in the various points of view, a number of themes recur. In the Alexander who looks out at us from the pages of books, we can discern a certain style, certain patterns of behaviour with which he relates himself to external reality, certain internal dispositions. The central question is: what are some of the more notable themes that guided him (Horowitz *et al.*, 1984; Luborsky & Crits-Cristoph, 1998; McDougall, 1985)? What can we deduce about the "script" that produced his inner theatre?

Let's take a closer look at Alexander the Great, starting with the external and moving within. The Alexander depicted in portraits and sculpted figures was an exceptionally handsome, clean-shaven man of below-average height for his day and age. Historical accounts tell us that he was in excellent physical shape, a splendid athlete with extraordinary coordination who enjoyed active exercises such as running and ball games. He also, however, enjoyed reading, music, and the theatre. He played the flute and the lyre, liked the more refined pleasures of poetry, but also favoured blood sports such as hunting. He was quick in dialogue and renowned as

Alexander as Pan: copy of marble sculpture by Lysippos, third century

a great orator. Intensely loyal to his friends and the men he led, he possessed passionate generosity, compelling charm, and personal magnetism. Although he had a number of intimate relationships, sexuality does not seem to have been of great interest to him. (To initiate him into sexuality as a youth, Olympias is supposed to have hired a *hetaira*, an elegant courtesan—an attempt that failed (Renault, 1975).)

Alexander was a complex mixture of light and shadows, impulsiveness and calm, selfishness and selflessness, virtue and vice. Although he was driven by a great need to be loved, he often acted in ways that evoked hatred. He was passionate in the extreme, often shifting rapidly from outbursts of affection to flare-ups of uncontrollable rage to bouts of depression.

A man of modest personal needs, Alexander lived like the other soldiers until near the end of his reign. Easy living and riches did not preoccupy him, although he enjoyed them when they came his way. According to most sources, his main driving forces were valour and glory. He was conditioned for success on the battlefield, having stretched himself to the limit from the outset. None the less, because he was an extraordinarily high achiever, he never seemed to be satisfied with what he accomplished. He was always longing for new achievements; to feel alive, to attain a sense of "flow", he needed to pursue conquest after conquest (Csikszentmihalyi, 1990).

Alexander was thirsty for knowledge, eager to learn, highly intelligent, and a great adventurer. He wanted to expand his horizons daily (or even hourly) and live life to the fullest. He was tempted by anything and everything unknown, liked to take risks, and enjoyed exploration. Highly imaginative and creative, he strove restlessly to reach unbounded territory and discover new and unknown things. He was driven by an incessant urge to succeed. But, as indicated by his life history, this need to win had a self-destructive component.

Internal imagery

The role models that occupied Alexander's internal world—lofty ones indeed—explain the "stretch goals" he set for himself. These role models included one ruler (Cyrus the Great), two gods (Zeus and Dionysus), one demi-god (Heracles), one epic chronicler (Homer), one hero (Achilles), and one philosopher (Aristotle). With these models as his guidelines, heroic emulation became Alexander's stimulus for action (Bosworth, 1988). Living up to these figures, and matching their exploits, would have been literally a Herculean task. Alexander must have felt enormous tension between where he perceived he was in his accomplishments and where he wanted to be. This tension between ego-*ideal* and ego would not have given him any peace, driving him forward at a relentless pace.

Alexander was very familiar with the exploits of Cyrus the Great and imitated many of his actions. The devotion Alexander expressed when visiting Cyrus's tomb illustrates how interested he was in the man. He was very much influenced by Xenophon's work *The Upbringing of Cyrus*. This Greek historian described Cyrus as a liberator, not a mere conqueror, because he respected the customs and traditions in each part of his growing empire. He made friends out of enemies and was hailed as a father by the conquered. Alexander would emulate this pattern of dealing with the conquered during the creation of his own empire.

The royal dynasty to which Alexander belonged traced their pedigree to Heracles. Since Heracles was a son of Zeus, the members of the noble family could (and did) style themselves Zeus-born. Alexander's mother emboldened him in his belief in his divine parentage from an early age—a belief that was strengthened by the affirmation of the Egyptian priests at Siwa (and by divine-origin prophecies that came out of Alexander's "propaganda" department). Alexander would flirt with his divine origins all his life. As mentioned, in some paintings Alexander was even implicitly portrayed as Zeus wielding a thunderbolt. The supreme god, Zeus was quite a role model to live up to. It was unimaginable to aim any higher, which must have put incredible pressure on Alexander.

As noted earlier, Olympias introduced Alexander to the cult mysteries of Dionysus when he was just a boy. It was believed that not only could Dionysus liberate people through wine and ecstatic frenzy, but he could also endow them with divine creativity. Because of that gift, he was the patron god of the arts, a domain of great interest to Alexander. It was said that Dionysus, having grown

Dionysus and Heracles: Greek red-figure vase

to manhood, wandered through many lands, carrying out a programme of conquest and civilization and promulgating the mysteries of his cult. Alexander, steeped in the mysteries of Dionysus, was curious about other religions and felt called to emulate this god by wandering through many lands, searching for (and finding) many signs of his presence.

If imitation is the sincerest form of flattery, Alexander's identification and rivalry with Heracles was about as flattering as you could get. The most popular of Greek heroes, Heracles was famous for his extraordinary strength and courage. Like Heracles, Alexander tried to perform arduous labours such as gaining entrance to impregnable rock fortresses and crossing the great Indus River (a feat that neither

Alexander in lion headdress: marble copy of bronze original, third century BC.
National Museum in Athens

Dionysus nor Heracles had ever accomplished). Like Heracles, he saw himself as having dual paternity (both an earthly and a heavenly father). Like Heracles he would transcend the boundary between the mortal and the divine (or so he hoped). Alexander's identification with Heracles helped him to overcome pain, hunger, thirst, heat, desperation, and great suffering with immense patience.

Frequently, Alexander portrayed himself garbed in a lion-skin helmet, in reference to Heracles' killing of the Nemean lion. He expected the same reverence of others: it was in part the refusal of Tyre's citizens to make a sacrifice to the god Melquart, whom he equated with Heracles, that prompted his awful vengeance on that city.

Alexander's actions were also guided by the spirit of Homer, who regularly appeared in his dreams. Alexander was such a devoted reader of Homer's great epic poems that the *Iliad* became his manual of war. He had a special copy of the poem made for himself that he took with him on his exploits. He carried it as he conquered two million square miles of the ancient world, and he slept with it under his pillow.

The *Iliad* deals with ancient Greek ideals of heroism, warfare, and glory in the context of a war against the city of Troy. Quite taken with the poem, Alexander could recite large sections of it by heart, imagining himself as the classic Greek heroes of yesteryear. His favourite hero of the epic was Achilles, from whom he was said to be a direct descendant through his mother. Throughout his life, Alexander would engage in a sort of rivalry with this hero, seeking to outdo Achilles' exploits with his own. Like Achilles, he tried to be a superhuman hero and warrior, exposing himself often to extreme danger during battle.

Guided by these formidable images in his inner theatre, Alexander was also much influenced by his interactions with Aristotle, his teacher and the greatest philosopher of his epoch. As we saw earlier, Aristotle's influence helped the younger man see (and value) what it meant to be a philosopher-king; Aristotle helped him acquire the intellectual skills needed to rule a great empire, stimulating his intellectual curiosity and spirit of discovery. Although Aristotle started out as an *actual* mentor to a young boy, he gradually became an *internalized* mentor to a powerful ruler, his ideas helping Alexander make inspired decisions during his campaigns.

All humans internalize the teaching of key people in their lives. The process of internalization starts with the parents and other early caretakers. The imagery evoked by the parents serves as the foundation on which other, later imagery is built. They stimulate the imagination of the developing child, shaping the script that will determine his or her inner theatre (McDougall, 1985; McDougall, 1989); they colour the themes that prevail in that script. As the infant matures, genetic and developmental components intertwine in a complex process of neural hardwiring in the brain (Lichtenberg, 1991; Lichtenberg *et al.*, 1992). Thus, the actions taken by early caretakers play a large role in determining later cognitive and emotional processes, behaviour patterns, and actions.

An oedipal victory: doing better than father

One of Alexander's most famous statements is, "I would rather live a short life of glory than a long one of obscurity" (Plutarch, 1992,

p. 220). This statement did not come out of thin air. From childhood onwards Alexander was trained to become a great ruler. Determined to make his mark, he worked hard throughout his short life to make sure that this expectation became a reality.

As many historians have testified, it was a compelling desire to succeed that made Alexander unstoppable. A core part of his character, his drive for success would not allow him to give up or even slack off. He refused to take no for an answer, because not to achieve what he set out to do was unthinkable. All someone had to do to motivate him was state that what he wanted to accomplish was impossible. That would get him up and running, eager to prove the other person wrong. The few times he failed to get what he wanted, he reacted with outbursts of rage and frenzied activity or (if he could not take "flight into action") depression.

Alexander's incredible level of achievement-motivation was clearly rooted primarily in his mother's support, although the influence of both parents was strong: they set very high standards for him, pushing him to be the best at everything (and modelling excellence in their own activities), and they gave him the best teachers available to help him meet their standards. It was Olympias, however, who was Alexander's staunchest supporter. Historians tell of a mother who assured her son that he had the ability to do anything, that he was far more capable than his father and could outdo him any time, that he was in fact a son of Zeus! Perhaps Freud had Alexander in mind when he noted that "If a man has been his mother's undisputed darling, he retains throughout life the triumphant feeling, the confidence in success, which not seldom brings actual success along with it" (Freud, 1917, p. 156).

Such over-stimulation can cause problems in children who discover that reality does not match the lofty fantasies created by their parents (Kohut & Wolf, 1978). Alexander was fortunate, however, in having other people—such as his father, his nursemaid, and his teachers—around him as stabilizing influences; they brought a solid dose of reality to his psychological equation. Alexander's giftedness did not hurt either; it helped him to come close to the high standards set for him.

In Alexander's adolescence, when the quarrels between his parents increased, he became Olympias's proxy and was often sent on missions to act out the wishes (be they explicit or implicit) of his mother. As proxy, he wanted to surpass his "unreliable" father and find favour in his mother's eyes. She had created an "unholy alliance" between herself and Alexander against King Philip (Willi, 1982, 1984). Given Alexander's position as only son and heir, he internalized the external struggle between his parents—a struggle that was eventually externalized again and acted out on a world stage (Lasswell, 1960). Throughout the struggle at home and the battles in the larger world, Alexander's need to succeed, to be better than everybody else, followed him like a shadow.

In particular, such a strong need to better his father, coloured (and ultimately blackened) Alexander's relationship with his highly successful father. As we saw earlier, at a young age Alexander said to his friends, "My father will forestall me in everything. There will be nothing great or spectacular for you and me to show the world" (Plutarch, 1973, p. 256). With King Philip always ruthless and successful in his own undertakings, Alexander felt a need to do even greater things just to prove his self-worth. Many of the early successes that were mentioned previously were linked to his father's accomplishments: Alexander was determined to tame his stallion, Bucephalus, in part because no one—not even his father—had yet managed that feat; his victory over the Thracian tribe and the triumph he felt when he established his first city, Alexandro-polis, was especially sweet given Philip's founding of a similar outpost after a victory; and Alexander's quest for divine honours was all the more urgent given that Philip had been granted divine honours during his lifetime (a mark of special distinction in Macedonian religious practice, usually given after death). In all these accomplishments, we can recognize Alexander's drive to surpass his father.

It was a complex relationship that Alexander had with his father—a relationship that mixed intense competitiveness with genuine admiration. The older man also served as a positive, constructive role model (Olympias's criticism notwithstanding), and Alexander must have relished the pride that his father took in his accomplishments (though that pride was sometimes tainted by ambivalence about his precocious son's behaviour). Whatever rivalry the older man felt, it did not prevent him, as we saw earlier, from giving Alexander the best education available. And whatever rivalry Alexander felt, the talented youth was eager not only to improve himself but also to please both his mother and his father. Only in his late teens did the relationship between Philip and Alexander sour and become dysfunctional.

At that time, we may assume that Philip started to worry about the extent of his son's ambition, to fear for his own throne. To have his subjects call Philip the general and Alexander the king must have been hard for the sovereign to bear. Likewise, it must have been difficult to watch himself (now partially lame and blind from battle wounds) become physically his son's inferior, a reality that was highlighted when his son saved his life. Alexander—with his athletic prowess, his intellectual precocity, his good looks, his competitiveness, and his sensational popularity with the soldiers— must have reminded the older man daily, simply by his existence, that his body was ageing, that his time was running out, that soon Alexander would want to take over the reins. Furthermore, it would not have escaped Philip's attention that parricide was a common pastime in ancient Greece (and one that a dangerous woman like Olympias might enjoy). No wonder Philip was tempted to shake up the original succession plan!

Compensatory striving

As successful as Alexander was, in both youth and adulthood, we have to wonder whether his need to win, to excel, was the manifestation of a solid sense of self-esteem or the outcome of more complex feelings. Was his drivenness the result of what psychologists call "constructive narcissistic development"—healthy self-love—or was it a cover for feelings of low self-worth (Kets de Vries, 1994)? Was Alexander troubled by the nagging doubt that he would never be good enough? Perhaps his parents, by carefully stacking the building blocks for a highly competitive spirit in their precocious son, had inadvertently planted in him the seeds of a fear that he could never reach the Olympian heights to which they aspired on his behalf. Alexander's constant craving for reassurance suggests that his extreme self-assuredness could have been indeed a "reactive" response, an attempt to overcome underlying feelings of inner doubt and insecurity. As we saw earlier, Alexander loved to be told about his achievements, a desire that seemed never to be adequately satisfied. His brief but extraordinary life shows us that a compensatory striving for superiority can lead to brilliant achievement, if that striving is backed by uncommon abilities.

Another factor that suggests that Alexander's internal life was troubled was his tendency towards "repetition compulsion"—that is, the compulsion to repeat certain activities over and over again, behaviour that is often based on painful, repressed memories. For some people, repetition becomes a form of mastery; the active repetition of various passively experienced disturbing life events gives a sense of control and creates a relative peace of mind (Loewald, 1971). To be more successful than his father was not enough for Alexander; he could not believe in a single instance of success—or two, or three. To convince himself of his superiority, he had to repeat the pattern over and over again (though the need for repetition would not necessarily have been conscious). Repetition compulsion accounts, in part, for Alexander's endless quest for new victories, his inability to slow down and consolidate his conquests.

The manic defence

Alexander was an extremely action-orientated person. Although this orientation contributed to his success, it eventually also caused him problems. The intensity of his need for action suggests that it had a "manic defence" quality to it, meaning that it was used to avoid thought and feeling. People troubled by depressive reactions, guilt, and isolation sometimes resort to a "flight into action" as a way of avoiding their demons (Etchegoyen, 1991; Klein, 1948), and Alexander seems to have been one of them. He sought new challenges to avoid the depressive anxiety that threatened to get the better of him. He was at his best when confronting an enemy or facing a seemingly impossible situation. Courting danger as if the first enemy he had to overcome was his own fear, he seemed to feel most alive in the middle of battle. Like activity generally, combat worked for Alexander as "counterphobic" therapy, holding his inner demons at bay. Thus, conquest gradually became an end in itself, not a means to an end.

After the incident at the Beas River, where he was forced by his men's reluctance to turn around rather than reach the Endless

Ocean, he was at an utter loss as to what he should do with the rest of his life. He was so overcome with disappointment and anger that he shut himself up and lay prostrate in his tent, refusing to eat (Green, 1991). He needed action to be able to function; it was as simple as that. The need for action also drove him after the death of his good friend Hephaestion: after a period of mourning, he retreated into a state of urgent movement, organizing a fleet and an army, giving ceremonious audiences, and participating in lavish evening banquets—activities undertaken to ward off depressive anxiety.

As a leadership style, action driven by need poses problems, whoever the leader is. In Alexander's case, it blinded him to the need for consolidating his many conquests; it deafened him to the advice of his Macedonian commanders, who (knowing that further conquests would be counterproductive) urged him to give top priority to the integration of his empire. A recommendation to engage in stable-state activities would only have increased his level of his anxiety, however.

Cyclothymia

Alexander's behaviour also possesses a cyclothymic quality—that is, a tendency towards radical mood swings (Goodwin & Jamison, 1990; Jamison, 1993; Kets de Vries, 2001b; Solomon, 2001). Alexander was known for his passionate temperament at both ends of the spectrum—his demonstrative expressions of affection and his voluble temper tantrums. During his impressionable youth, these extremes of mood probably went largely unchecked, given the autocracy of Philip's court.

People who have cyclothymic tendencies face a strange mixture of feelings: a well-being characterized by sparkle and exhilaration juxtaposed against emptiness and loneliness. These up- and down-swings, which recur with disturbing frequency, often result in behaviour that has (as Alexander's did) a larger-than-life quality.

Research has shown that affective disorders are inheritable, and cyclothymia is no exception: there is a genetic component to cyclothymic behaviour. Given Olympias's erratic behaviour, we can hypothesize that Alexander inherited certain cyclothymic qualities from her. Stressful life events (and Alexander had enough of those) also seem to play a role in the manifestation of this disorder (Goodwin & Jamison, 1990).

Cyclothymics in an upswing tend to possess a remarkable attractiveness that is often described as charisma. They exhibit abundant physical and mental energy, unbridled enthusiasm, eager gregariousness, intense feeling, a sense of destiny, a strong belief in themselves and their ideas (bordering on the grandiose), persuasiveness in convincing others of their point of view, willingness to go where others dare not go, optimism, heightened alertness and observational ability, courage, willingness to take risks (bordering on the imprudent), impatience, unpredictability (and subtle changeability) in mood, and shortened attention span.

As mentioned before, Alexander was at his best in situations of crisis. It was those situations that sent him into an upswing. In battle, for example, he felt truly alive, felt a sense of exaltation and rapture, a heightened sense of reality. And the intoxication he felt when "high" was contagious, as is the case for cyclothymics generally. His positive mood state inspired and motivated his men to do great things; it drew other people to him and held them in his sway. It is this aspect of cyclothymia that ties the disorder to charisma and helps those who possess (or are possessed by) it reach positions of leadership. The enhanced liveliness of cyclothymics on the upswing—in combination with their uninhibited gregariousness, their interpersonal charm, their ability to find vulnerable spots in others and to make use of them, their perceptiveness at the subconscious or unconscious level, and their social ease—creates a special interpersonal and group dynamic that can positively affect performance, eliciting exceptional efforts from those affected.

There is a darker side to this behaviour, however. For every upswing there is a downswing; there is a threat of imminent depression, with its accompanying feelings of melancholy, deadness, and hopelessness, and with its tearfulness, suicidal thoughts, and self-deprecatory and self-accusatory behaviour. Those darker moods can be just as contagious as the enthusiasm of an upswing. Even the *positive* moods of cyclothymics can lead to trouble, however. Because of the larger-than-life quality of their behaviour, misdirected cyclothymics can be like the Pied Piper, leading people astray, pursuing directions that turn out to be costly to themselves and to their constituency. In addition, cyclothymics in an extremely manic phase are prone to explosive outbursts of rage that alienate others, and to alcohol and drug abuse.

Many aspects of Alexander's behaviour fit with what we know of cyclothymia. Alexander was the Pied Piper of antiquity, taking his troops on campaigns of epic proportions through formidable terrain. His charisma was such that, until the turning point at the Beas River, his men were prepared to follow him anywhere, any time; they were prepared to face any challenge as long as Alexander was at the helm. His ability to challenge his people, to motivate them, survived even their disastrous trek through the Makran desert, where many of the men perished. However, whenever circumstances forced Alexander into inactivity, his depressive side appeared and he retreated into his tent in a melancholic funk, reappearing only when he could take his troops on a short campaign as an antidote to the depression (Solomon, 2001).

Like other cyclothymics, Alexander was no stranger to outbursts of rage. We saw evidence of his temper in the fight with his father at the marriage banquet, his towering rage at Thebes over being labelled a dictator (and the resulting destruction and enslavement of the city), his vindictive response to the unwillingness of Tyre to hand over their city (and the resulting crucifixion of its fighters), his rage over the Persians' non-acceptance of him as a legitimate king—let alone divinity—(and the resulting destruction of Persepolis), and his anger over the ingratitude of the Macedonian veterans.

Rage that is centred around problems of self-esteem, as Alexander's was, is called "narcissistic rage". When cyclothymics experience setbacks as narcissistic injuries—in other words, injuries to their self-esteem—their positive feelings can quickly change into outbursts of disappointed rage. In Alexander's case, those outbursts occurred on a vast, dramatic stage, in circumstances that gave him absolute power over life and death. Thwarting the sovereign could be devastating, especially when alcoholic intoxication exacerbated his dysfunctional self-control.

Cleitus was an old-guard commander in the Companion Cavalry who had fought under Philip and (as the brother of Alexander's old nursemaid) had known Alexander his whole life. In one battle he had even saved Alexander's life. At a banquet just before

Cleitus was to be sent to assume the governorship of Bactria, disaster struck. The banquet was in celebration of the Macedonian feast-day for Dionysus, and everyone over-indulged in wine. At one point during the festivities—perhaps in response to court flatterers, who specialized in praising Alexander while denigrating his father—Cleitus became infuriated over Alexander's "oriental ways" and (knowing of the royal rivalry) taunted him with the claim (he couldn't have found a better trigger mechanism to fury) that Philip had been a much greater man than he was. To add insult to injury, he scoffed that Alexander had been carried to success by his Macedonian troops through no contribution of his own and mocked Alexander's pretension to be the son of Zeus-Ammon. Alexander, increasingly angry himself, threw an apple at Cleitus, whose friends hurriedly carried him out of the hall. Cleitus struggled free, however, and returned to the hall to deliver a new insult. Now completely enraged, Alexander grabbed a spear and stabbed Cleitus through the heart. The older man fell dead at Alexander's feet (Arrian, 1971; Plutarch, 1973).

Cleitus, therefore, learned about his king's mood swings the hard way. Although he watched Alexander erupt into rage, he did not live to see the whole story. According to some historical sources, Alexander would immediately have killed himself with the same spear if his officers and friends had not restrained him from doing so. Totally disgusted with himself, he then took to his bed in a misery of self-revulsion and depression. For three days he refused all food, drink, and comfort (Arrian, 1971; Plutarch, 1973). Cynics could interpret this behaviour as a ploy to gain the army's sympathy and forgiveness for the murder of a popular commander so that Alexander's officers would not mutiny against him. However, going to bed was certainly not the most effective way to prevent mutiny; Alexander, savvy in his dealings with subordinates, could have designed a more effective ploy had he set out to do so. More likely, he was stricken by guilt, especially since Cleitus was an old family friend and a kinsman of his beloved nursemaid.

On that occasion, Alexander overcame his depression with the help of his entourage, who offered acceptable rationalizations, and a priest of Dionysus, who proclaimed that the god had possessed Alexander with madness to punish Cleitus for a slight on his feast day. Only after three days of constant petitions and persuasions on the part of both priest and entourage did Alexander finally rouse himself from his bed to begin living again. A review of this incident reveals a man who was capable of making horrendous mistakes when inebriated and in the heat of anger, and who experienced dramatic changes in mood.

Relationships

As we have seen, Alexander's early relationships with his parents, his paternal grandmother, his nursemaid, his teachers, and his role models (some real, some imagined) affected his development profoundly. His ongoing relationship with these figures, and his later relationships with women and men (especially his three wives and his friend Hephaestion) were also important to who he was and how he saw himself.

In sensual matters, Alexander has been both portrayed as homosexual and "defended" from such "allegations". One group of scholars accepts a reputed disinterest in women, while the other tries to deny it. Neither group, however, gives proper attention to Alexander's circumstances or to the social realities of antiquity. In those days, and in that region, an erotic affection for women did not preclude an equal affection for men. As was typical of his era and culture, Alexander (who is known to have had a number of lovers, both male and female) appears to have been comfortably bisexual.

Relationships between men and women in ancient Greece and Macedonia, particularly within the upper classes, differed radically from those of today. In the world of Greek antiquity, which largely shared Aristotle's belief that women are imperfect forms of men, a man's essential, deep relationships were typically with other men. The fact that Alexander's primary affective relationship might have been with another man is not only unsurprising, then, but also predictable. Adding to the complexity, the Macedonian royal house practised polygamy (though not all of Greece did), further complicating male–female relationships.

Research evidence suggests that biological factors contribute significantly to the modification of sexual choice. Environmental experiences within the nuclear family of childhood, however, can also leave a legacy. Researchers studying male homosexuality in

Hephaestion: bronze head attributed to Polyecleitos

contemporary society note that many homosexuals have a father who, for various reasons, is not an ideal object of identification and a mother who does not encourage male sexual identification in her son. Such a family constellation has been identified as a factor that can lead to gender confusion (Green & Blanchard, 1995; Levine, 1993). Alexander scholars who see the great king as a homosexual use such evidence to support their case, pointing out that his family constellation fits the model.

That is faulty logic, however. The above model does not *necessarily* apply to the ancient Greeks, because its underlying nature–nurture paradigm is embedded in a specific, contemporary sociocultural matrix. The ancient Greeks had no word that corresponds to our "homosexual", suggesting that the ancients viewed one's choice of bed partner as merely a choice, not a reflection of deep-seated psychological preferences.

Traditional male relationships in Greece generally involved an adult male and a boy. The model for homoerotic attachments in antiquity was that of elder *erastes* (lover, pursuer, and active partici-

pant) and younger *eromenos* (beloved, pursued, and passive partici-
pant), a model not unfamiliar to Alexander. One of his biographers,
Mary Renault, notes that a Persian eunuch named Bagoas was
frequently cited as his *eromenos* (Renault, 1975, 1988). Given the
sexual practices of the day, Alexander's relationship with his best
friend Hephaestion was unusual not because it was homoerotic,
then, but because the two partners were of the same age. Furthermore, a number of historical sources suggest that Alexander was
still Hephaestion's lover at the age of thirty, an age when most
Greek men would have selected a younger lover. It was possible in
ancient Greece, however, for two young men of roughly the same
age to be sexually involved without that attachment being frowned
upon (Green, 1991; Lane Fox, 1994).

Despite the downright ordinariness of homoerotic relationships
among males in ancient Greece, it is undeniable that Alexander's
exceptionally close relationship with his mother *could* have had a
great impact on the development of his sexual preferences. As
mentioned earlier, most historians agree that Alexander idolized his
mother. When the child, and later the young man, had conflicts
with his father, she always took his side and defended him.
Predictably, when the rupture occurred between Olympias and
Philip, Alexander returned the favour and took her side. So intri-
cate and lasting a bond was formed with his mother that it could
have prevented other women from playing a significant role his life.

Alexander's opinion of the institution of marriage might have
affected his interest in the opposite sex as well. With his parents'
marriage as a role model, he cannot have yearned for the marital
bed. Alexander spent his childhood watching the relationship
between his mother and father deteriorate, watching his parents
become virtual enemies of one another. Naturally, this left a great
impression on the young boy, stuck in the middle of the feud. And
as this feud progressed, it was only natural (given the intensity of
the relationship he had with Olympias) that he came strongly under
the influence of his mother. A counterbalancing identification
with his father was lacking, given his father's frequent absences on
military campaigns and the strong rivalry between father and son.

Alexander's closeness to his childhood nurse, the queen mother
Eurydice (his paternal grandmother), and Sisygambis (the mother of
King Darius, whose granddaughter was his second wife) illustrates

the importance of other maternal figures in his life. His nurse-maid and his grandmother, in particular, must have been important in his personal development. It is interesting to note that he seemed to be attracted to middle-aged or elderly women. And women liked him back. When Sisygambis had an opportunity to return to Persia, for example, she chose to stay with him. Unfortunately, very little is known about his relationships with his wives and mistresses (of whom he is thought to have had two), although it is thought that Alexander treated all the women in his life with great respect.

Although Alexander enjoyed women generally, it was the strong emotional attachment to his mother that remained the most intense throughout his life. She was always on his mind, even when he was far away. He sent her spoils from his conquests, and they corresponded actively during all his military campaigns. In the letters Alexander received from her, she came up with one request after another, hatching the most outrageous schemes and asking for his help. His love for his mother was such that, as he once supposedly said, "One tear of hers would outweigh all the complaints Antipater [his regent in Macedonia] had about her" (Hammond, 1993, p. 200). On the other hand, he is also supposed to have said, in regard to his mother's demands, that he had to pay a great deal of rent for his nine months' lodging (Fildes & Fletcher, 2001, p. 17).

Alexander had his mother with him in spirit always, but he had many childhood friends with him in body on his ambitious endeavours. He seems to have invested much of his emotional capital in these friends during the early years, given the difficulties at home; and they were a source of support in adulthood as well. An indication that these friends were important to his mental health is found in the fact that they were given senior command positions as his campaigns progressed. It was his childhood friend Hephaestion, however, who enjoyed Alexander's primary affective attachment, as we have seen. He, not any of Alexander's three wives or the eunuch Bagoas, was the king's real "significant other" (quite apart from any sexual involvement). They could always be found together, and those who did not know them were often confused as to which of the two was Alexander. Olympias was extremely jealous of their relationship, but even she was unable to sow discord between the two men.

Psychologists give the label "twinship" to the relationship that lies behind friendships of this intensity. Twinship can be viewed as a special form of narcissistic link, protecting an individual from feelings of dependency and helplessness. Clinical research has shown that in the "alter ego" of the twinship experience, the "other" is experienced as being just like the self. Individuals who have experienced narcissistic injuries—injuries that are self-esteem-linked—often look for others like themselves to feel whole again, to feel reinforced and supported (Kohut, 1971, 1977). Narcissistically vulnerable people seek others to give them attention, "echoing", and approval. The "twin" in the form of Hephaestion represented the "other" whose qualities coincided with Alexander's and whom Alexander could use for the confirmation of the existence of the self.

An illustration of this twinship process in action can be seen in the first encounter of Alexander with Darius's mother, Sisygambis. When they met, Hephaestion was with him, and both men were very simply dressed. Sisygambis began to prostrate herself before Hephaestion. In great distress when she realized her error, she again prostrated herself—this time before the king. Alexander stepped forward and lifted her up, then ". . . remarked that her error was of no account, for Hephaestion, too, was an Alexander—a 'protector of men'" (Arrian, 1971, p. 123).

Hephaestion, as alter ego, became Alexander's sounding board, playing an important, affirming role in the king's life. The "mirroring" he provided gave him a dose of psychological security. The two of them spent lots of time together, philosophizing on life, sharing ideas, and discussing the future, so we can assume that Hephaestion was of great assistance in helping Alexander overcome his occasional bouts of self-doubt and depression. Likewise, we can also assume that he played a very important role in reality-testing, confirmation of self, and the attainment of insight.

Alexander liked to compare their relationship to that of Achilles and Patroklos, Achilles' most intimate friend. When they visited Troy, Alexander laid a wreath on the tomb of Achilles while Hephaestion laid one on that of Patroklos (Plutarch, 1973). This analogy continued when the king cut his hair in honour of Hephaestion's death, just as Achilles had done when Patroklos died. Alexander's mourning for his good friend's death is thought by some to have been the only time in his life that he showed genuinely deep grief and affection. His behaviour during and after the funeral was as depressive as could be imagined, with serious suicidal overtones. It was as if part of Alexander had died. Some historians—those with a psychological bent—have speculated that Alexander's last battles were strategic fiascoes not because of his mistakes but because of a lack of will to live after the death of Hephaestion.

Megalomania

Leaders need a solid dose of narcissism to attain positions of leadership (Kets de Vries, 1989; Zaleznik & Kets de Vries, 1975). However, narcissism typically becomes more pronounced once leadership and a position of power have been attained. Because the ability to deal with the psychological pressures of leadership shows the real person, the acid test for leaders comes once they are at the helm. Can they keep their narcissistic proclivities in check? Can they deal with fame with a certain amount of equanimity, or does it go to their head?

Given the unequal relationship between leaders and followers, some leaders become victims of their own success, falling prey to hubris. Hubris is a recurrent theme in leadership, for the obvious reason that excessive pride and arrogance often accompany power. The predictable offshoot of uncontrolled narcissism, this expression of dysfunctional self-love is indicated by excessive self-reference and self-centredness. Hubris exacts a high cost: leaders prone to excessive narcissism see only what they want to see—a process reinforced by the followers' idealization of them (Kernberg, 1975; Kohut, 1971, 1977). How does this work? Leaders in the grip of hubris typically become exploitative, callous, and over-competitive, frequently resorting to excessive use of depreciation when the behaviour of followers is not to their liking. They are prone to outbursts of rage, behaviour that fosters submissiveness and passive dependency in followers. Followers whose critical function has been stifled tell the leader what they think the leader wants to hear.

Leaders who are the victim of hubris take for granted that they can transform the rules made for lowly followers. They feel that

Alexander's entry into Babylon: detail from a painting by Charles le Brun

because their needs are special, they can do whatever they want—even transgress. This feeling of entitlement adds to the failure factor in leadership. Hubristic leaders, insensitive to the wants and needs of others, take advantage of their followers to achieve their own ends. Loving no one but themselves, they see themselves as superior and attribute unique, special qualities to themselves. This excessive grandiosity is often reflected in exhibitionistic tendencies, recklessness, and outsized ambitions. It also contributes to faulty decision-making given the quality of information that they receive.

Other expressions of pathological self-love include an over-dependence on admiration by others and an incapacity for gratitude. Admiration is taken for granted rather than appreciated by hubristic leaders, who themselves dish it out only sparingly. Such leaders often begrudge others their successes or possessions, feeling that they themselves are more deserving (American Psychiatric Association, 1994; Millon, 1996). The sense of superiority they feel is often interrupted by dramatic bouts of insecurity or inferiority, however. Although they present themselves as absolutely self-confident and independent, that is often a front for very different feelings (including the worst fear of all: that of being found merely average). Especially when they are feeling insecure, they may retreat into a world of their own, becoming myopic, opinionated, and deaf to the advice of others. This inner theatre probably features a chronic state of emptiness, of aloneness. Plagued by a sense of the meaninglessness of life, hubristic leaders seek comfort in endless admiration from others and in their efforts to control others (and thereby "own" the success of others, which otherwise would cause envy).

Many of the qualities ascribed to the narcissistic personality seem to apply to Alexander. Certainly, he was no stranger to narcissism: he liked to be in the limelight, and he wanted and expected to be admired. In his case, however, he really was an exceptional person—superior, if what one measures is accomplishment. Successful beyond anyone's imagination, he achieved impossible things. In other words, much of the praise that he reaped from others was deserved. As indicated, however, the acid test for a successful person is whether reality-testing starts to become impaired by success.

For a leader in Alexander's position—and with his list of successes—it would have been difficult to avoid becoming the victim of hubris (Kets de Vries, 1993, 2001b). The larger his territory grew, the less likely it would have been that reliable checks and balances (such as the advice of trusted counsellors) would affect him. With sycophants the order of the day, he had a veritable "Greek chorus" to echo his opinions. As Alexander's delusions of grandeur increased (if the word "delusion" is correct here, given his incredibly successful campaigns), he seemed to live more and more in his own world; and soon (because of the incredible power he wielded) his reality became others' reality. A mutual regressive process occurred, as it always does between hubristic leader and dependent followers, giving rise to inappropriate behaviour and detouring people from reality (Freud, 1921). Eventually, very few people were courageous enough to stand up to Alexander and challenge his false reality. Those who dared to did so at their own peril, the murder of Cleitus being a terrifying example.

Some historians have suggested that it was after his visit to the Oasis of Siwa—where he consulted the oracle of Zeus-Ammon— that Alexander began to lose touch with reality. The oracle told him that he would "get what his heart desired" (Green, 1991), which he took to be a reference to his desire for divine parentage. Alexander wanted others to recognize that all his achievements were due to his having been touched by divinity. Perhaps, as the stakes in his far-reaching ventures rose—his fear of failure climbing with them— he sought in his link with the gods a divine shield of invincibility. Fighting increasing battle fatigue and the perils of the flesh, he must have wanted to be worshipped as a god as a way to come to grips with his own mortality.

Alexander's tragedy as his power increased was a growing isolation and loneliness—the result of the distance from his fellow men (and thus from reality) that his unbroken ascent to absolute power demanded. Where before he had been very close to his troops, now he had become more and more distant from them— even from the Macedonians. As "yes-men" increasingly populated his retinue and an atmosphere of flattery began to infiltrate his court, he no longer wanted to be challenged by his Macedonian Companions, with their traditional Macedonian frankness, and he lost his sense of playfulness.

Alexander's key officers were concerned by their leader's deterioration. The Macedonian army, steeped in an archaic feudal form of democracy characterized by (among other things) freedom of speech, detested Alexander's drift towards oriental despotism, his adoption of Persia's dress code and protocol (which assumed infallibility of the king), his efforts to ingratiate himself with the Persians, and his attempts at forced integration between Persians and Macedonians. For hundreds of years the Greeks and Macedonians had made fun of the despotic habits of the Persian monarchy, only to see their own king now insisting on the extreme ceremonial practice of *proskynesis* (obeisance and prostration), a ceremony that the Greeks reserved for the gods.

His officers disliked intensely the oriental cult protocol, with its endless taboos and rituals; they detested seeing Alexander parade around in outlandish robes, and they resented being forced to be on intimate terms with the effeminate nobles they had just defeated. And with Alexander playing the role of a Persian king (if not the son of Zeus-Ammon, wearing purple robes and ram's horns), it became increasingly difficult to have casual interaction with him. The easy give-and-take of the past—the banter that had characterized

Persian court ritual: palace relief, Persepolis

relationships previously—had given way to the stifling formality of Persian court ritual. This increasing formality was exacerbated by the numbers game: an increasing number of Persians had been inducted into his army and had never known him in different settings. The Macedonians feared to become an isolated minority— a group of people that would be expendable.

Things came to a head, as we saw, at the Beas River. Although only General Coenus had the courage to speak up and tell Alexander that it was time to stop, his troops clearly wanted to go home; they had had enough and were mutinous. Finally his insatiable thirst for conquest was halted, at least temporarily. The incident at the Beas River can be viewed as a psychological landmark: Alexander finally realized his estrangement from his troops. No longer able to simply cajole his men into action (or even "bribe" them with ever-increasing spoils of battle), he feared that he was losing his basic touch. No wonder he was so upset. No wonder his reactions were those of rage and depression.

As noted earlier, another symptom of dysfunctional narcissism is envy (whether conscious or not). At times almost overwhelming, this emotion is often accompanied by manifestations of spite and vindictiveness. As we think back to Alexander's early adulthood, his envy of his father and his impatience to assume the role of king stand paramount. We can see examples of vindictiveness too, as when Alexander bridled under the chiding of his teacher Leonidas concerning the young man's wastefulness of incense—a slight that he nursed for more than a decade before sending the older man eighteen tons of the substance! Although that could be seen as a practical joke, there was probably more to it. Alexander seems to have been a person who would remember those who had slighted him.

Excessive narcissists deal with envy through a variety of means, including idealization, devaluation, and exploitation. In idealization, narcissists set on a pedestal those who are successful. Soon, however, that idealization turns into devaluation: narcissists "pollute" their potential sources of envy, making less of their successes. In exploitation they seek to inherit the benefits of others' success that they see as rightly their own. It is as if such people experience those around them only as idols, enemies, or fools.

Further indicators of excessive narcissism are an inability to empathize with others and an inability to make substantive relational commitments. Narcissists may express extraordinary love for mankind, but they are generally uninterested in and uncommitted to actual personal relationship. Moreover, their inability to establish deep relationships with others may contribute to sexual difficulties. Although Alexander was able to make relational commitments, as his friendship with Hephaestion indicates, as time went by his circle of friends narrowed dramatically. He dropped many of his original friends and Companions by the wayside, and he executed some. Soon only Hephaestion and Alexander's geographically distant mother helped him maintain human connectedness.

Narcissistic personalities typically deteriorate when they get older, and Alexander was no different with a life-style that accelerated the process. The combined effects of unbroken victories, unparalleled wealth, absolute and unchallenged power, extraordinary physical stress, alcoholic bouts, and isolation began to take their toll. Alexander became increasingly domineering and grandiose. His temper became more and more unpredictable: at the slightest provocation he would erupt in rage. Furthermore, he was

Alexander: copy of statue by Lysippus, marble. Inscription: "Earth is my footstool! Zeus, you can keep Olympus!"

increasingly suspicious, ready to believe any rumour of perfidy, whatever the source. The execution of his most capable commander, Parmenion, and the commander's son were consequences of such suspicions.

Paranoia

The paranoid personality has its origin in a basic lack of trust. Such a lack frequently originates in a family constellation that produces an unpredictable, hostile environment. Someone brought up in such an environment needs to be vigilant, always prepared for sudden deception and attack. The result is an adult who is extraordinarily sensitive to incidences of hostility, criticism, and accusation (Cameron, 1963; Horowitz et al., 1984; Meissner, 1978; Shapiro, 1965).

Hypersensitivity and feelings of insecurity or inferiority often lead to delusions of superiority and grandiosity. Children who are expected to perform impeccably, and who are undeservedly punished when they fail to do so, may develop elaborate fantasies as a way of enhancing injured self-esteem. Those secret fantasies may then eventually evolve into delusions. While a trusting person can also develop grandiose delusions, his or her dominant mood is euphoria. A paranoid person with persecutory delusions, on the other hand, is predominantly suspicious.

The most common form of delusion is the persecutory type—delusion rooted in a pervasive, unwarranted suspiciousness and mistrust of people. It usually involves a single theme or a series of connected themes, such as being cheated, followed, poisoned, conspired against, spied on, or obstructed in the pursuit of long-term goals. Persons with persecutory delusions are often resentful and angry, and they may resort to violence against those they believe to be hurting them. They substitute an internal threat—the threat they carry within them—for an external one and take action against that external threat, thereby gaining a modicum of control. The need to control people and circumstances reflects the low self-esteem that frequently lies at the core of paranoia.

Paranoiacs turn within for protection from perceived dangers, unable to trust the counsel of others. Inclined to misinterpret the incidental actions of others as signs of deception and malevolence, they prefer to be the makers of their own fate, free of entanglements and obligations. Fractious and abrasive irritability often comes to the fore in such people, and isolation is the ultimate consequence. Alexander's treatment of some of his close Companions can be seen as the result of paranoia, the exception being Hephaestion.

A comforting, constant mother image is the best preventive for paranoia, but we can only guess at the degree to which Olympias provided that image to her son. However, what we know about her outsized temperament, her mood swings, and her religious practices make constancy seem unlikely. Oscillating behaviour patterns tend to leave a young child (and later an adult) with a feeling of inconstancy. When children cannot be sure what to expect from their mother, the environment seems full of uncertainty. They may feel strongly drawn to their mother but at the same time feel persecuted and threatened, fearing that she may betray or leave them.

We know that Alexander did not lack support. None the less—given palace politics—his family and other intimates must have instilled in him a solid dose of suspicion, for the simple purpose of survival. Rumour-mongering and treason at the highest levels of Greek and Macedonian society were part of *realpolitik*; they could not have escaped Alexander's attention. Over time, an initially healthy suspicion of others may have become part of the young man's habitual mode of cognition.

While it is unlikely that a paranoid disposition was Alexander's predominant style, the exposed position he was in, especially as an adult, would have aggravated whatever paranoid disposition he possessed (Kets de Vries, 1995). He needed to be hypervigilant and hypersensitive to survive. With the possibility of murder ever present, he needed to watch for cues that would betray the hidden motives of others. He had to be on guard from hostile invasion, both literal and figurative.

Individuals prone to paranoid reactions tend to distance themselves, resorting to defences such as reaction formation, denial, and projection. In Alexander's case, reaction formation (or the tendency to transform an unacceptable feeling or thought into its opposite) helped him to deal with his anxiety-producing dependency needs. He denied his deeply-felt dependence, transforming it instead into staunch independence. Fearing psychological "engulfment" by his mother, he distanced himself as only a campaigning commander can: by staying away for years on end. Alexander's comment on meeting the unfettered philosopher Diogenes—"If I were not Alexander, I would be Diogenes"—may also point to the tension he felt between dependence and independence. Having been exceptionally dependent on his mother early on, he feared renewed dependence and craved independence. Dependence would always be equated with helplessness and vulnerability for him. When he found himself helpless and forced to change his position at the Beas River, the resulting anxiety precipitated a depressive episode.

Like all people with paranoid tendencies, Alexander also resorted to the denial defence, avoiding awareness of reality when it became too painful. His problems with denial intensified as he gained ever more success and glory. Increasingly, he saw only what he wanted to see, denying unacceptable reality. And his courtiers, eager to share in his success, were more than willing to oblige.

Alexander also used projection as a defence. People with a paranoid disposition generally have a hypervigilant, combative interactive style, but they do not always like that characteristic. To protect themselves from recognizing their own unacceptable impulses, they project what they are feeling on to others. As Alexander grew older, he seemed to project his resentment and anger on to others, suggesting that he was unable or unwilling to take responsibility for his feelings. At other times he would resort to rationalization, excusing his actions by blaming them on divine intervention, thus denying responsibility. The battlefield provided an ideal outlet for the hostile impulses that troubled him. What better way to deal with aggression than by vanquishing a foe? Although Alexander used his anger with outstanding results against his enemies, he was not always as successful at dealing with anger outside battle situations, as we have seen.

For Alexander, in a position of extreme power for which many opponents would cheerfully have murdered, the problem of distinguishing reality from fantasy must have been difficult. As the saying goes, "You don't have to be paranoid to know that people are after you." As indicated earlier, a bit of paranoia would have been a useful survival strategy. He knew, after all, that his father had been murdered by a trusted follower; in fact, that deed haunted Alexander all his life. And yet, becoming more and more convinced of his divinity as the years and victories progressed, he found it increasingly difficult to accept differences of opinion. Any disagreement over policy with his senior commanders could trigger a paranoid reaction. The consequence of such a paranoid outlook was predictable: an atmosphere of sycophancy.

Alexander's paranoia revealed itself over the issue of *proskynesis*. As has been mentioned earlier, it was a means of expressing extreme obeisance that the Macedonians reserved for gods and the Persians granted to kings. Perhaps Alexander would have been willing to forego *proskynesis* if he had been a "normal" mortal. After all, the Greeks and Macedonians had always made fun of the "barbarous" habits of the Persians, believing that mortal men did not deserve such reverence. But because he viewed himself as possessing the godhead, the rite was deadly serious. Callisthenes, his court historian and the nephew of Aristotle, invited Alexander's wrath by ridiculing this procedure and insisting on a strict separation between human and divine honours. Alexander accused him of plotting against the sovereignty and had him executed.

In 330 BC he accused a brilliant cavalry commander, Philotas, of conspiring to plan his death and had him executed. To prevent a blood feud, he also had Philotas's father, Parmenion—his major general—executed. What a sad reward for a person who was so instrumental to Alexander's success! From that day on, assuming that he could not trust even his closest Companions, he used the divide-and-conquer method, never concentrating too much power in the hands of one commander.

Although there were undoubtedly many people who would have liked Alexander to be out of the way, he took his precaution to an extreme. As his advisers grew less and less willing to state their mind, for fear of the consequences, his system of reality-testing crumbled. Eventually, with no one willing to challenge his self-created reality, his palace became a house of mirrors.

CHAPTER NINE

The aftermath

As we saw earlier, before Alexander started his campaign his senior advisers Antipater and Parmenion had advised Alexander to first put his house right in Macedonia and establish a line of succession. He disregarded their advice, however, and embarked on his expedition unmarried and childless, leaving his whole political and military structure almost totally dependent on his survival. His heroic self-exposure—his desire always to be the first in battle, to fight upfront—was a constant invitation to disaster. The many times he was wounded confirm the frailty of the organizational and military machine he had created.

After his death, Alexander's generals fell to quarrelling about how to divide his legacy. Although his conquests were greater than those of anyone before him, he had made no real effort to integrate and consolidate the governments of the lands he had taken. Because putting in order the enormous empire that he had won was not the most *challenging* task he could undertake, he chose not to do it—a decision that had almost as much to do with his time period, perhaps, as with his personality. As a result, for the next four decades or more, the empire that Alexander had created and held together by sheer force of personality was ripped apart in his generals' violent power struggles.

Alexander falls into in the category of individuals who shaped the world as we know it. He changed the history of civilization—no mean feat! The first great conqueror to reach Greece, Egypt, Asia Minor, and Asia as far as western India, he set the limits of what was considered to be the inhabited earth. Not until the voyages of the Portuguese and Spanish in the late fifteenth century would Europeans be convinced that they had finally explored farther than Alexander had.

The world itself—not just its boundaries—was changed by Alexander. Before Alexander, world civilization had been dominated by eastern cultures—by Persians, Egyptians, Babylonians. Alexander shifted the spotlight once and for all. From his day on, the western societies of the Romans and the Greeks would carry the torch. From victory to victory, from triumph to triumph, he created an empire that made him a myth. He was that rare figure who became a hero in his own lifetime.

Let us review some of his accomplishments:

1. He brought Greek ideas, culture, and life-style to the countries that he conquered and assured the expansion and domination of the Hellenistic culture, which, together with Roman civilization and Christianity, constitutes the foundation of what is now called Western Civilization.
2. He marched for eleven years over 20,000 miles and never lost a battle.
3. He united an area of over twenty-two million square miles.
4. He adopted Persian dress and customs, married Bactrian and Persian princesses, and required thousands of his Macedonian and Greeks to wed Persian women.
5. He proclaimed himself god-king in Egypt and in Greece for the alleged purpose of unifying his empire.
6. He took scientists along on his expeditions to gather data about biology and geography.
7. He made Greek the prevailing language of the Near East for all matters of government, learning, and commerce.
8. He established many new colonies and cities (*seventy* of them named after him in his honour!).
9. He started a great experiment in acculturation by sending many children of Near Eastern families to Greece to be educated.

10. He trained and used Persians in his army.
11. He used Greeks, Macedonians, and Persians in his administration in an attempt to unite East and West.
12. He revolutionized international trade by setting up a common system of currency for the entire realm. (The economic system that began to take shape after Alexander's reign remained virtually unchanged until the Industrial Revolution of the nineteenth century.)

CHAPTER TEN

Leadership lessons from Alexander the Great

Alexander also taught the world a number of important lessons on leadership. Through his example, contemporary leaders in business and politics can learn much about what leaders should (and should not) do. The major lessons he taught us should be applied every day in offices and conference rooms throughout the world:

1. Have a compelling vision
2. Develop a creative strategy responsive to enemy strengths
3. Create a well-rounded executive role constellation
4. Model excellence
5. Encourage innovation
6. Manage meaning to foster group identification
7. Encourage and support followers
8. Invest in training and development
9. Consolidate gains
10. Plan for succession
11. Create mechanisms of organizational governance

Have a compelling vision. Alexander's actions demonstrate what can be accomplished when a person is totally focused, when he or she has a magnificent obsession. His behaviour confirms yet again the importance for leaders of having a clear, well-defined *vision*; effective leaders must be able to clearly convey what the existing situation is and where they want people to be headed. From early on, Alexander knew what he wanted to accomplish. His leap on to the beach after crossing the Hellespont and his statement about becoming the ruler of Asia made that quite clear. By making such a dramatic gesture, he spoke to the collective imagination of his people. His army was going to make things right; they were going to demand retribution for Xerxes' slight to the Greek world. Alexander's rhetorical skills helped them buy into this greatest of all adventures. Alexander knew where he was going and how to get there. Unfortunately, he did not know how or when to stop (to the great confusion and dissatisfaction of his troops).

Develop a creative strategy responsive to enemy strengths. Alexander was one of the most brilliant military strategists of all time. He had a great vision, yes, but he knew how to make that vision reality. His use of strategy is unsurpassed in the annals of history. On the battlefield he knew how to take maximum advantage of any situation, adapting quickly to the tactics of his opponents. He was comfortable in any battle situation, from standard combat to guerrilla warfare, and he was always prepared for the unexpected. He *maintained an excellent information system* and knew how to interpret his opponents' motives. He certainly informed himself of the competition. Because he was a master at coordinating all parts of his military machine, *perfect execution* on the battlefield became his competitive advantage. Furthermore, no other military leader has ever used *speed and surprise* with such skill.

Create a well-rounded executive role constellation. Alexander also knew how to shape a committed team around him. He carefully selected his key staff members. Subsequently, he created an "executive role constellation" by which each of various commanders could build on the others' strengths (Hodgsdon *et al.*, 1965). While Parmenion played an essential role on the battlefield and Antipater, his regent in Macedonia, kept his home base in order, his other key commanders superintended their particular domains. Their teamwork created the extraordinary coordination that made for Alexander's success on the battlefield. Only in later years did his relationships with his key people deteriorate.

Model excellence. Alexander set the example of excellence with his leadership style; he walked the talk. As mentioned earlier, he was not an armchair general. He led his troops quite literally. He did not *talk* their battles; he *fought* their battles. During the early years, unwilling to enjoy the comforts of his position, he lived the soldier's life, sleeping in simple tents and eating mess food. When his troops went hungry or thirsty, he went hungry and thirsty; when their horses died beneath them and they had to walk, he did the same. This situation changed only when he was seduced by the luxury of Persian court life and became obsessed with the divinity question.

Encourage innovation. Alexander knew how to encourage innovation. Because of his deft deployment of the phalanx, his support for and reliance on the creativity of his corps of engineers, and his own logistical acumen, his war machine was the most advanced of its time. He knew the importance of understanding his adversaries, so he paid a great deal of attention to military information systems and used reconnaissance to maximum advantage. Alexander's creativity and innovation were not limited to the military field, however. His curiosity about biology, zoology, and medicine, and his support for the scientists on his expeditions, led to further developments in these areas of research.

Manage meaning to foster group identification. As has been noted, Alexander was a master at the management of meaning. He had a propaganda machine, and he used it effectively. His oratory skills, based on the simple language of his soldiers, had a hypnotic influence on all who heard him. As an exemplary charismatic leader, he made extensive use of myths, metaphors, analogies, and stories, evoking powerful cultural symbols and eliciting strong emotions. When he felt that his case needed strengthening, he knew how to use his diviners to reframe various incidents as tokens of destiny; and he used symbols and rituals (such as sacrifice to the gods) to great effect. These meaning-management actions, combined with his talent at leading by example, fostered strong group identification among his troops, motivating the men to give exceptional effort.

Encourage and support followers. Alexander was a praise-singer. He knew how to encourage his people for their excellence in battle in ways that encouraged further and greater excellence. He routinely singled people out for special attention and recalled acts of bravery performed by former and fallen heroes, making it clear that individual contributions would be recognized. He paid attention to his men's needs, visiting and helping the wounded, arranging for elaborate ceremonies for the fallen (and providing for their widows and children), and rewarding his troops handsomely. He possessed what I like to call a *"teddy bear" quality*, meaning that he had the ability to be a "container" of the emotions of his people (Kets de Vries, 2001a).

Invest in training and development. Extremely visionary for his day, Alexander spent an extraordinary amount of time and resources on training and development. He not only trained his present troops but also looked to the future by developing the next generation, schooling young Persians in the ins-and-outs of Macedonian warfare and striving to bring Greek language and mores to Asia.

Consolidate gains. Three of Alexander's most valuable lessons were taught not through his strength but through his weakness. The first of these is the need to consolidate gains. He didn't *put the right systems into place* to integrate his empire. Alexander never savoured the fruit of his accomplishments. Captive to the demons in his inner world, he could not rest and enjoy but felt compelled to go ever forward. It was as if he had no choice. His temperament, personal development, and historical moment combined to make him who he was: a man destined to succeed in battle and to win a vast empire. They also limited him, however, forming the walls of a psychic prison that constrained him from consolidating his domains. Conquest may be richly rewarding, but a leader who advances without ensuring the stability of his or her gains stands to lose everything.

Plan for succession. Another lesson that Alexander taught (and the second that he taught by omission) is the need for a feasible succession plan. Alexander was so focused on his own role as king and aspiring deity that he could not bring himself to think of a future without him. As a result, vultures tore his vast empire apart after his death. Power is an easily ignited explosive that must be transferred with care.

Create mechanisms of organizational governance. The final lesson that the case of Alexander illustrated (again taught by omission) is the paramount importance of countervailing powers. Unchecked power creates hubris, contributing to decline and fall. Leaders have the responsibility (although it may be too much to ask from them) to put proper mechanisms of organizational governance into place. Checks and balances are needed to prevent the abuse of power and faulty decision-making. Alexander began his reign as an enlightened ruler (particularly comparing his rule to the practices of his age), encouraging participation by his Companions and others. But, like many rulers before him, he became addicted to power. As time went on, applause from his audience was the only thing he could tolerate. With candour disappearing, he began to live in a world of his own. Reality-testing suffered, with very negative consequences to his quality of decision-making. Eventually, very few of his immediate circle were willing to contradict him. They would only tell him what he wanted to hear. Only a crisis, such as what happened at the Beas River, would create a temporary mirror of reality. But getting increasingly out of touch contributed to the lack of consolidation of his empire and his missing of the "Endless Ocean".

It would be difficult to say which of these lessons is the most important, because an empire's (or an organization's) needs change throughout its history. Although all these lessons are important, Alexander taught the last three most forcefully, emphasizing their importance with the crumbling of his empire. Although his realm was huge and wealthy, his hubris was greater still. Feeling invincible and unstoppable, he neglected the gains he had already achieved and gave no thought to what would happen to his lands and his people if he were to die. He shared the view that would later be expressed by one of his successors in the field of empire-building, Louis XIV. "*Après moi le déluge*", Louis said, apparently unconcerned about what he would leave behind. And perhaps there is something to that view: the playwright Molière, a contemporary of the French king, said (through a character in his play *Le Misanthrope*), "The greatest folly of all is wanting to busy oneself in setting the world to rights."

NOTES

There are five historians from antiquity whose work on Alexander is still at least partially in existence: Arrian, Plutarch, Diodorus, Justin, and Curtius. Although these writers lived and wrote hundreds of years after Alexander's death, we have little choice but to rely on their works, despite their distorting filters, because the many accounts of Alexander's life that were written by his contemporaries and associates have been lost to us forever.

Arrian's account, which is generally considered the best and most reliable, is the one I use most frequently here for my descriptions of the historical Alexander. It was written more than four hundred years after Alexander's death in Arrian's role as an official of the Roman Empire. Arrian is the only one of the five authors mentioned in the previous paragraph who included in his work the names of his sources and his reasons for relying on them. His main sources were the memoirs written by Ptolemy, one of Alexander's generals, and the writings of Aristobulos, a Greek architect who travelled with Alexander and worked closely with him over many years; Arrian also used works of Nearchus, who was Alexander's admiral and life-long friend. Ptolemy and Aristobulos wrote their accounts, produced independently of each other, in response to their growing dissatisfaction over the slanted, anti-Alexander stories that were being circulated and encouraged in Macedonia by Cassander (who had usurped the throne and had had Alexander's mother, wife, and son murdered) and in Athens by the Athenian educational establishment. Arrian's clear and straightforward writings rely upon these very reputable primary sources that have themselves been lost to us.

Of the four remaining authors, Plutarch is preferred. Unfortunately, his contributions need to be used with caution, as he is not an unimpeachable source. He wrote in the first century AD., relying on sources that have since been revealed to be suspect (such as letters that were supposedly written by Alexander but were later proved not to be). Plutarch also, in his later years, revised some of his earlier work on Alexander. He portrayed the later Alexander more negatively in those revisions, a change suggesting that he had come under the influence of the anti-Alexander propaganda.

The writings of Curtius, Diodorus, and Justin are of dubious quality. All of these authors relied upon suspect sources for their works on Alexander. Justin's main source was a relatively obscure person named Trogus, who did not like Alexander. Diodorus and Curtius, though the earliest writers on Alexander (having penned their accounts in the first century AD), produced works full of mistakes and rich in fictionalized writing. Each seems to have relied a great deal on another writer, Cleitarchus, whose works are largely lost to us. Cleitarchus was thought to have been a contemporary of Alexander and was therefore assumed, for many years, to be a reliable source. Writers such as Cicero and Strabo, however, believed him to be untruthful in describing events in Alexander's life, and most present-day historians reject as unreliable any writings about Alexander based on Cleitarchus's works.

In this short book I have used many different sources to understand what Alexander was all about. All passages shown in quotation marks derive from an ancient text or inscription. Because there exists a great deal of confusion concerning certain episodes and events in Alexander's life (combined with many different interpretations of such events), I have tried to be parsimonious, focusing on episodes in his life where most authors are in agreement. For an excellent discussion of the problems of historical sources concerning Alexander, see the bibliography contained in Bosworth's *Conquest and Empire: The Reign of Alexander the Great*.

REFERENCES

American Psychiatric Association (1994). *Diagnostic and Statistical Manual for Mental Disorders, DSM-IV* (4th edn). Washington: American Psychiatric Association.

Aristotle (1988). *Athenian Constitution, Eudemian Ethics, Virtues and Vices*, Vol. 20 (H. Rackham, Trans.). Cambridge, MA: Harvard University Press.

Arrian (1971). *The Campaigns of Alexander* (A. d. Selincourt, Trans.). Harmondsworth: Penguin.

Ashley, J. R. (1997). *The Macedonian Empire: The Era of Warfare under Philip II and Alexander the Great, 359–323 BC*. New York: McFarland & Company.

Baynham, E. (1998). *Alexander the Great: The Unique History of Quintus Curtius*. Ann Arbor: The University of Michigan Press.

Bion, W. R. (1959). *Experiences in Groups*. London: Tavistock.

Bosworth, A. B. (1988). *Conquest and Empire: The Reign of Alexander the Great*. Cambridge: Cambridge University Press.

Bury, J. B., & Meiggs, R. (1983). *A History of Greece to the Death of Alexander the Great*. London: MacMillan.

Cameron, N. (1963). *Personality Development and Psychopathology*. Boston: Houghton-Mifflin.

Cawkwell, G. (1981). *Philip of Macedon*. London: Heinemann.

Csikszentmihalyi, M. (1990). *Flow: The Psychology of Optimal Experience*. New York: Harper and Row.

Diodorus, S. (1992). *Books 16–17*, Vol. 8 (C. H. Oldfather, Trans.). Cambridge, MA: Harvard University Press.

Dupuy, T. N. (1969). *Military Life of Alexander the Great of Macedon*. New York: Watt, Franklin.

Erikson, E. H. (1958). *Young Man Luther*. New York: W. W.Norton.

Erikson, E. H. (1963). *Childhood and Society*. New York: W. W. Norton.

Etchegoyen, R. H. (1991). *The Fundamentals of Psychoanalytic Technique*. London: Karnac.

Fenichel, O. (1945). *The Psychoanalytic Theory of Neurosis*. New York: W. W. Norton.

Fildes, A., & Fletcher, J. (2001). *Alexander the Great: Son of the Gods*. London: Duncan Baird.

Freeman, C. (1999). *The Greek Achievement*. London: Penguin.

Freud, S. (1905). Fragment of an analysis of a case of hysteria. In: J. Strachey (Ed.), *S.E., 7*. London: The Hogarth Press and The Institute of Psychoanalysis.

Freud, S. (1917). A childhood collection from Dichtung und Wahrheit. In J. Strachey (Ed.), *S.E., 17*. London: The Hogarth Press and the Institute of Psychoanalysis.

Freud, S. (1921). Group psychology and the analysis of the ego. In: J. Strachey (Ed.), *S.E. 7*. London: The Hogarth Press and the Institute of Psychoanalysis, 1953.

Freud, S. (1929). Civilization and its discontents (J. Strachey, Trans.). In: J. Strachey (Ed.), *S.E., 21*. London: Hogarth Press and the Institute of Psychoanalysis.

Fuller, J. F. C. (1989). *The Generalship of Alexander the Great*. New York: Da Capo Press.

Goodwin, F. K., & Jamison, K. R. (1990). *Manic-Depressive Illness*. New York: Oxford University Press.

Green, P. (1991). *Alexander of Macedon*. Berkeley: University of California Press.

Green, R., & Blanchard, R. (1995). Gender identity disorders. In: H. I. Kaplan & B. J. Sadock (Eds.), *Comprehensive Textbook of Psychiatry*. Baltimore: Williams and Wilkins.

Hammond, N. G. L. (1993). *Sources for Alexander the Great*. Cambridge: Cambridge University Press.

Hammond, N. G. L. (1998). *The Genius of Alexander the Great*. Chapel Hill: University of North Carolina Press.

Hodgsdon, R. C., Levinson, D. J., & Zaleznik, A. (1965). *The Executive Role Constellation*. Boston: Harvard University Press.

Hogarth, D. G. (1977). *Philip and Alexander of Macedon*. New York: Ayer Company.

Horowitz, M. J., Marmor, C., Krupnick, J., Wilner, N., Kaltreider, N., & Wallerstein, R. (1984). *Personality Styles and Brief Psychotherapy*. New York: Basic Books.

Jamison, K. R. (1993). *Touched with Fire*. New York: The Free Press.

Kazantzakis, N. (1982). *Alexander the Great* (T. Vasils, Trans.). Athens, OH: Ohio University Press.

Keegan, J. (1988). *The Mask of Command*. New York: Penguin.

Kernberg, O. (1975). *Borderline Conditions and Patholigical Naricissism*. New York: Aronson.

Kets de Vries, M. F. R. (1989). *Prisoners of Leadership*. New York: Wiley.

Kets de Vries, M. F. R. (1993). *Leaders, Fools, and Impostors*. San Francisco: Jossey-Bass.

Kets de Vries, M. F. R. (1994). The leadership mystique. *Academy of Management Executive*, 8(3): 73–92.

Kets de Vries, M. F. R. (1995). *Organizational Paradoxes* (2nd edn). London: Routledge.

Kets de Vries, M. F. R. (2001a). *The Leadership Mystique*. London: The Financial Times/Prentice Hall.

Kets de Vries, M. F. R. (2001b). *Struggling with the Demon: Essays in Individual and Organizational Irrationality*. Madison, CT: Psychosocial Press.

Klein, M. (1948). *Contributions to Psychoanalysis*, 1921–1945. London: Hogarth Press.

Kohut, H. (1971). *The Analysis of the Self*. New York: International Universities Press.

Kohut, H. (1977). *The Restoration of the Self*. Madison, CT: International Universities Press.

Kohut, H., & Wolf, E. S. (1978). The disorders of the self and their treatment: an outline. *International Journal of Psycho-analysis*, 59: 413–426.

Lamb, H. (1945). *Alexander of Macedon: The Journey to World's End*. New York: Doubleday.

Lane Fox, R. (1994). *Alexander the Great*. New York: Viking/Penguin.

Lasswell, H. (1960). *Psychopathology and Politics*. New York: Viking Press.

Levine, S. (1993). Gender-disturbed males. *Journal of Sexual Marital Therapy*, 19: 131.

Lichtenberg, J. D. (1991). *Psychoanalysis and Infant Research*. New York: Lawrence Erlbaum.

Lichtenberg, J. D., Lackmann, F. M., & Forshage, J. L. (1992). *Self and Motivational Systems: Toward a Theory of Psychoanalytic Technique*. New York: Analytic Press.

Loewald, H. W. (1971). Some considerations on repetition and repetition compulsion. *International Journal of Psycho-analysis*, 52: 59–65.

Luborsky, L., & Crits-Cristoph, P. (1998). *Understanding Transference: The Core Conflictual Relationship Theme Method*. Washington: American Psychological Organization.

McDougall, J. (1985). *Theaters of the Mind*. New York: Basic Books.

McDougall, J. (1989). *Theaters of the Body*. New York: W.W. Norton.

Meissner, W. W. (1978). *The Paranoid Process*. New York: Jason Aronson.

Millon, T. (1996). *Disorders of Personality: DSM IV and Beyond*. New York: John Wiley.

Plutarch (1973). *The Age of Alexander: Nine Greek Lives* (I. Scott-Kilvert, Trans.). Harmondsworth: Penguin.

Plutarch (1992). *Moralia*, Volume 4 (F. C. Babbitt, Trans.). Cambridge, MA: Harvard University Press.

Renault, M. (1975). *The Nature of Alexander*. London: Penguin.

Renault, M. (1988). *The Persian Boy*. New York: Vintage Books.

Shapiro, D. (1965). *Neurotic Styles*. New York: Basic Books.

Solomon, A. (2001). *The Noonday Demon: An Atlas of Depression*. New York: Simon & Schuster.

Stewart, A. (1993). *Faces of Power: Alexander's Image and Hellinistic Politics*. Berkeley: University of California Press.

Willi, J. (1982). *Couples in Collusion: The Unconscious Dimension in Partner Relationships*. Claremont, CA: Hunter House.

Willi, J. (1984). *Dynamics of Couples Therapy*. London: Jason Aronson

Zaleznik, A., & Kets de Vries, M. F. R. (1975). *Power and the Corporate Mind*. Boston: Houghton Mifflin.

INDEX